Creative Historical Thinking

To check =

1. John Cleese lecture on creativity
2. Lakoff + Johnson, Metaphors We Live By
3. Sample Dutch calendar
4. Locate a short story that represents time as non-linear

Creative Historical Thinking offers innovative approaches to thinking and writing about history. Author Michael J. Douma makes the case that history should be recognized as a subject intimately related to individual experience, and positions its practice as an inherently creative endeavor. Douma describes the nature of creativity in historical thought, illustrating his points with case studies and examples. He asserts history's position as a collective and community-building exercise, and argues for the importance of metaphor and other creative tools in communicating about history with people who may view the past in fundamentally different ways. A practical guide and an inspiring affirmation of the personal and communal value of history, *Creative Historical Thinking* has much to offer to both current and aspiring historians.

Michael J. Douma is Assistant Research Professor at the McDonough School of Business at Georgetown University.

history = "related to individual experience
• inherently creative endeavor } gets to his thesis,
re: metaphor (2-}

chapters = Scaffolding of my instruction

Questions =
• What does it mean to think about history creatively?

Key = "metaphors are instruments of creativity in historical thinking" (1), he discusses on 2 + 3,
" must understand the influences on our interpretations of history (sources of knowledge, metaphors in use) (4)

Creative Historical Thinking

Michael J. Douma

Routledge
Taylor & Francis Group

NEW YORK AND LONDON

First published 2018
by Routledge
711 Third Avenue, New York, NY 10017

and by Routledge
2 Park Square, Milton Park, Abingdon, Oxon, OX14 4RN

Routledge is an imprint of the Taylor & Francis Group, an informa business

Library of Congress Cataloging-in-Publication Data
A catalog record for this book has been requested

ISBN: 978-1-138-04883-6 (hbk)
ISBN: 978-1-138-04885-0 (pbk)
ISBN: 978-1-315-11284-8 (ebk)

Typeset in Goudy
by Apex CoVantage, LLC

Contents

Imagining the Past by Sloane Shearman

Figures

Preface

I want to claim my ideas as my own, but I'm certain that most of the time my ideas did not begin with me. The truth is, a historian can never cite all of their sources. Much about the way a person interprets the world is shaped by their experiences in childhood. By middle age, they've experienced too much to remember where they first encountered an idea. Wherever my ideas came from, I know they were shaped in discussions with friends and family, and with students and colleagues.

Many of the ideas in this book I have presented in lectures on American history at Florida State University, the University of Illinois-Springfield, and James Madison University. I have also presented them in guest lectures in a dozen other places. Because I am trained in the history of the United States, most of the examples in the book come from American history, rather than say European, African, or Asian history. This is an accidental feature of the book, whose true aim is not to explain American history per se, but to explain something about the discipline of history itself.

In choosing to write about history, I owe a great debt to those who have come before, but I also owe it to the readers of this book to not just repeat what others have written. Many books on the nature of history and historical thinking explain the development of historical study and the successes and failures of its various theories.[1] Today, an absolutely astounding number of new publications on history appear each year, and many of them are quite good, but only a few of these books show the creative side of history. To me, this is a great problem. I see history as a creative and engaging art, and I want others to view it this way as well.

Practical history research guides typically include short sections covering epistemology (the philosophy of knowledge) and historiography (historical views of history). But the main purpose of most of these books is to serve as manuals for students who are thinking about historical research for the first time. These texts march students through terminology and the specific steps of research, analysis, interpretation and writing. With few exceptions, however, they remain detached and uninspiring.[2] I have never met a professional historian who claims that their inspiration came from a textbook or a research guide. Step-by-step guides to historical research remind me of a driver's education teacher in a classroom, explaining how to drive a car by going over the function of the gas pedal and brake, the turn signal, and the gas gauge. The only way you can really learn to drive is from experiencing the feel of the road.

Likewise, I think that historians are made in libraries and in the archives, and I believe that research guides are of little value if they treat historical research skills as a boxed good, independent from actual historical practice. A good history book is one that inspires its readers to get to work doing history. Young historians should learn from the examples of their teachers and share in their curiosity and passion for history, but if they are to think like historians, they need to develop their own stride and their own voice.

I respect my own great teachers, and foremost among them Bill Cohen and Bob Swierenga. My inspirations also include the physicist Richard Feynman, who encouraged us to confront conventional wisdom and to look at the world from a new point of view, and the comedian John Cleese, whose lecture on creativity has been a motivating force for me. I dedicate this book to the young scholar who is looking for answers. I welcome correspondence from readers of this book, and I will do my best to respond to any questions about history or the history profession.

I've had many discussions that have helped this book develop. Thanks to Trevor Burrus, Daniel Moseley, Bill Glod, Lael Weinberger, Rob Faith, Hans Eicholz, Scott Shubitz, Kevin Currie-Knight, Michael O'Leary, Suzanne Sinke, Richard Cytowic, Frederick Turner, Michael Watson, Herman Paul, Christopher Griffin, Todd Zywicki, Jason Brennan, Lauren Brennan, Marian Eabrasu, Carson Young, Lydia Ingram, and Anders Bo Rasmussen. I thank Sloane Shearman for the art in Figure 0FM.1, Xavier Macy for images in the book, and Martha King for work on the index. I thank my Facebook feed for the many comments and leads on my historical musings. Thanks also to Gracie Pater, Pascal Bandoch, Henry P. Bigfellow, and everybody named Kevin. There would be a lot fewer Kevins without you. For inspiration, I'd like to thank D.J. Wolffram, Chris Arndt, Richard Bell, and Peter Boltuc.

Making history is a personal exercise, and some would even say that all history is really just autobiography, since we are always projecting our own experiences onto the past. For these reasons, among others, I make no apology for the personal nature of the content to follow or for the use of the personal pronoun "I."

Notes

1. Works of this kind are numerous, so a few prominent examples should suffice: Patrick Gardiner, ed., *Theories of History* (New York: The Free press, 1959); Leonard M. Marska, *The Nature of Historical Inquiry* (Holt, Rinehart and Winston, 1970); Joyce Appleby, Lynn Hunt, and Margaret Jacob, *Telling the Truth About History* (New York: W.W. Norton & Company, 1994); John Burrow, *A History of Histories: Epics, Chronicles, Romances & Inquiries from Herodotus & Thucydides to the Twentieth Century* (London: Penguin, 2009, original, Allen Lane, 2007). For those looking for traditional history methods books, I can recommend John Lewis Gaddis's *The*

Landscape of History and Stephen Davies' *Empiricism in History* (New York: Palgrave, 2003). For graduate students I still prefer the somewhat more difficult classics by Collingwood, Carr, and Nevins. John Lewis Gaddis, *The Landscape of History: How Historians Map the Past* (Oxford: Oxford University Press, 2004); R.G. Collingwood, *The Idea of History* (1945); E.H. Carr, *What Is History* (1961); Allen Nevins, *The Gateway to History* (1938).

2. Examples include John Tosh's *The Pursuit of History*, which also is a primer on various approaches to history. Similar to Tosh are Michael J. Galgano, J. Chris Arndt, and Raymond M. Hyser, *Doing History: Research and Writing in the Digital Age* (Boston, MA: Wadsworth Publishing, 2012 [original 2007]) and Jeremy Black and Donald M. MacRaild's *Studying History* (London: Palgrave, 2007), which is a good, comprehensive guide.

Introduction

One day, when visiting a friend's house, I picked up a plastic toy shovel in the hallway, pretended I didn't know what it was, placed it on my head and said: "Hey Allison, look at my hat."

Allison, my friend's 6-year old daughter, laughed, and I handed her the plastic shovel while asking her a question: "OK, what do you think it is?"

She thought for a second, then put the toy under her foot, and said: "Look, it's a sandal with a pointy toe."

When I got the object back, it was my turn again. I demanded that the toy was neither a hat nor a sandal, but was actually a canoe paddle, and I mimicked the motion of paddling a canoe. This game went on through another ten or twelve rounds of laughter before we got tired and gave up.

When I encounter historical evidence, I play a similar game in my mind. "What is this thing?" I ask myself about an old letter, a piece of pottery, or a photograph. And, "where does it fit in the story I want to tell?" "Maybe," I think, "this piece of evidence confirms a story as I has imagined it, or maybe it changes the story entirely." Certainly, the evidence could be interpreted in many ways, but what is the best interpretation?

Thinking about history is a creative game that we all play from time to time as we try to imagine possible interpretations for past events. Imagination is required to give meaning to even the most obvious historical artifacts. We create stories when we see pattern and meaning in the observed world. The past is what happened. But history, the interpretation of the past, cannot be written without creativity.

If, however, you think about creative disciplines taught in school, you might think of music, art, or writing, but not history. For a variety of reasons, history as taught in the classroom tends to be nothing like a free-flowing game of interpretation with a kid at play. In the classroom, history is often taught as a set of facts associated with a nationalist or political narrative. As teachers struggle to get through a certain amount of content in a semester, there is little time for them to explore their own curiosity about the past or to inspire students to do the same. The creative element hardly has room to flourish. The discipline suffers.

The idea that history is a creative discipline, however, might seem threatening. If a shovel can be mistaken as a shoe, or a hat, then it stands to reason that some of the facts of history that we have learned might be wrong. Any rational, intelligent person has to admit that of course we could have all sorts of things wrong about history, although I imagine that a large number of people would feel bothered by the idea that much of written history is guesswork. People like certainty, even if it is an illusion.

But I want to push back against this uncomfortable uncertainty, for the sake of honesty and truth. If history is a creative discipline, do I mean then that everybody gets to decide whether George Washington was the United States' first president, or whether the Norman invasion of England actually happened?[1] My answer is yes, we all get to decide whether we want to believe something or not. It would be unwise to deny such established and evidenced facts of history, but there are plenty of facts and stories that are worth debating and that call out for a creative historian to interpret with new evidence in new ways, so as to provide a better explanation. It is an obvious truth that we know things about the past because we follow the evidence to a conclusion. If we casually accept all of the historical facts we encounter, we probably wouldn't be able to entertain a coherent picture of the past. Instead, we sort through facts and build narratives that make sense and that explain things.

This book hopes to remedy the problem of uncreative history education while inspiring new ways of thinking about the past for professional and non-professional historians alike. It is a book about what it means for historians to think creatively, and it is a primer on historical thinking, with plenty of examples that may help you improve your powers of creative historical imagination. The book is divided into four sections. An opening section, Chapters 1 through 3, presents an argument about how history should be seen as a creative discipline. The second section, Chapters 4 through 7, is designed specifically for college students who want to learn how to read, write, and network as creative historians. The third section of the book, Chapters 8, 9, and 10, presents some examples about how creativity can be incorporated into the classroom. The final section, Chapters 11 through 14, elaborates on the consequences of creative history.

The organizing claim of this book is that metaphors are instruments of creativity in historical thinking. A metaphor is "at its simplest, a way of proceeding from the known to the unknown."[2] For historians, metaphors are crucial because they help us to imagine and represent the unknown past by reference to what is known in the present. Philosophers George Lakoff and Mark Johnson explain that metaphors are more than expressions of language, they structure our thought, they highlight similarities between one thing and another, and they provide understanding.[3] While we share many basic metaphors, each person uses metaphors derived from a fundamentally unique set of experiences to make sense of the world. People who can draw on a greater number of experiences—a greater range of knowledge—can employ a larger array of metaphors to explain past events.

Historians recognize that metaphors are not just interpretive tools that we apply after we have located the facts. They actually help determine the historical facts we seek and the ways we organize those facts. For example, if our metaphor for a person's life is a journey, we will seek facts that fit traditional elements of a journey: a beginning, a challenge, a turn or fork in the road, a goal. But if our metaphor for life is a game, we will seek facts that correspond to scoring points, living by the rules, or working through periods of activity. Biographies written with those differing metaphors might tell quite different stories. Although each person visualizes the past in his or her own way, discussion of past events is still possible if we accept that our metaphors are rooted in similar experiences, grounded by the same rules of natural science and logic. If, however, we only have one metaphor to put to use, we only have one way of perceiving the world. To a hammer, everything looks like a nail. To a paranoid person, everything is a threat. To an ideologue, everything fits a political narrative.

The centrality of metaphors for creative historical thought might lie deep in our very nature. Cognitive scientists and philosophers who defend what is known as the "embodied mind thesis" believe that we understand the world through metaphors that are rooted in basic concepts of the body moving through space.[4] Some of our basic thought is literal, such as in the statement "this is a coffee cup." But much of our thought, and all of our abstract thought, is metaphorical and imaginative. To say that we should "have coffee" means that we should meet up, or take our time. We speak metaphorically when we say that coffee is our drug, our liquid energy, our lifeblood.[5]

Of course, we can make literal statements about the past, but without metaphors, we cannot present interpretations of historical facts. Unconsciously, we categorize the data we observe in the world and seek patterns that can be expressed as metaphors. Lakoff and Johnson explain that "We acquire a large system of primary metaphors automatically and unconsciously simply by functioning in the most ordinary of ways in the everyday world from our earliest days."[6] In our common language and common culture, we agree on hundreds of primary metaphors such as "important is big," "happy is up," "bad is stinky," "similarity is closeness," "difficulties are burdens," "change is motion," "knowing is seeing," "causes are physical forces," "categories are containers," and "time is motion." We then blend these primary metaphors to create conceptual metaphors. Working from our sensorimotor domains, we create mental imagery that can be used to interpret subjective experiences, like history.

To be clear, metaphor in creative historical writing is not just a choice; I believe it is an inevitability—we literally cannot avoid metaphorical thought in thinking about the past. This is why historical writing is saturated with metaphors. For an example of the ubiquity of metaphors in historical thought, consider a passage from a book called *Frederick the Great and the Rise of Prussia*, by D.B. Horn. The first sentence reads "The rise and fall of empires is one of the few constants in history and has attracted attention from classical times to the present day." The primary metaphors at work in this sentence, "rise" and "fall," draw on our spatial sense and stand for the changes that contribute to the existence or non-existence of an empire. The word "attracted" is also a primary metaphor comparing human interest to a force pulling two things together. The phrase "from classical times to the present day" reflects a metaphorical understanding of time as distance. Interest in the rise and fall of empires doesn't literally attract people, nor do empires literally rise and fall; and time, of course, does not literally exist in physical form.[7] When Horn continues in the following paragraph to write about the tensions and interplay of "Great Powers" in Europe, he is treating the European theater as an arena of physical forces. But this is one of many possible metaphors one could employ to describe European politics of the time, and thus it is a creative choice. If the author chose another metaphor—perhaps, say, "youth and age" instead of "rise and fall"—he could have written about how the Roman Empire came to an end through a natural process of aging. Then, we might be inclined to think not of the "Fall of Rome" as if it were an unexpected tragedy, but rather as a natural process. In other words, the choice of metaphor will shape how we treat the events.

Well-used metaphors imbue historical writing with more than layered meaning; they also add substance and style. In his influential book *The Death of the Past* (1969), the English historian J.H. Plumb chose an easily understood architectural analogy to describe the collapse of the Christian past as a guide to modern civilization. Plumb wrote:

> [The] old majestic theme of man's fall and salvation, has collapsed. Rubble, broken arches, monuments crumbling to dust, roofs open to the sky litter this world of thought and loom forebodingly against the horizon.[8]

To get his point across, Plumb could have merely said that with secularization in the West, traditional religious stories had lost their importance. But his chosen metaphor provides a visual image that we can hold on to. Peering through the collapsed roof of a cathedral, looking up to the sky, we see the process of twentieth-century secularization in metaphorical terms. We can imagine Plumb's historical image.

To think about history in new, creative ways, we need to have varied experiences that provide us with new metaphors to employ. Arthur Koestler's *The Act of Creation* (1964) shows us how this process of discovering new ideas through metaphorical thinking might work. According to Koestler, much of our thought processes belong to sets of associated knowledge. Associations of knowledge exist as bundles in discrete symbolic domains. We might think of our knowledge of things like geometry, plumbing, Calvinism, or baseball as isolated little worlds, each with its own clear system of associational knowledge. Koestler invented the term "bisociation" to describe how we can understand something simultaneously through two "self-consistent but habitually incompatible frames of reference."[9] Unlike associative skills, which allow us to gain competence in one domain, bisociative skills allow us to connect, combine, destroy, and rebuild across domains. Creativity, especially in writing history, derives from bisociative thinking. The creative act, says Koestler, is the "discovery of hidden analogies," the:

> bringing into consciousness of tacit axioms and habits of thought which were implied in the code and taken for granted; the uncovering of what has always been there. . . . It does not create something out of nothing; it uncovers, selects, re-shuffles, combines, synthesizes already existing facts, ideas, faculties, skills.[10]

An image from Koestler's book (Figure 0.1) illustrates his concept of bisociation of frames of reference. Two frames of reference, such as music and architecture, can be connected. The creative result is that we can see one thing in terms of another, such as in the phrases "architecture is frozen music" or "all the world's a stage, and all the men and women merely players." We might think also of the points of bisecting frames as words in a sentence with double meaning: one frame shows the literal path of a sentence, and the second holds the meaning of a pun. In other words, puns and most jokes consist of entangled frames. The moment of discovery, when we recognize how two things fit together, leads to the "Aha!" response. Humor and surprise have this same origin, and it is no coincidence that when we discover something new, we say, "Isn't that funny?"[11]

Metaphors are more consistent and more powerful when the two objects they link can be mapped onto each other to show correspondences in their structures. This property of relational correspondence has been called "isomorphism" or "systematicity."[12] Models select information to communicate.

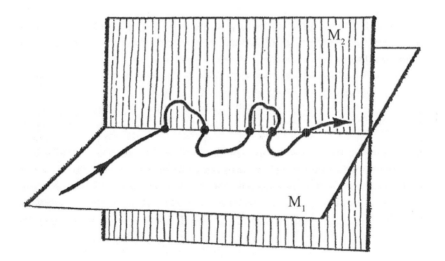

Figure 0.1 Koestler's Multiple Frames of Reference

The frames interact to highlight metaphorical thought leading to creativity.

They highlight the essential point and also create new categories to investigate in the proposed relational structure. Douglas Hofstadter writes that "perceptions of isomorphism create meanings in the minds of people" and they are the source of "Eureka!" moments in the production of new mathematical knowledge.[13] Isomorphism appears in the universal, logical, and mathematical, but also in the particular, contingent, and historical. We seek analagous structural elements to match historical data to our conceptual metaphors.

Our metaphors for explaining history come from our own experiences, so the greater number and variety of experiences we have and can recall, the more likely we are to recognize pattern or meaning in the world around us. The lesson for historians, then, is that we need to increase the variety of our experiences so that we can recognize more possible ways to interpret historical developments. History is not a set of associated knowledge; rather, it is by its nature a discipline of bisociative knowledge. In other words, history is not a set of facts, but a form of interpretation that relies on fitting together various kinds and pieces of knowledge. Historical knowledge isn't one set of knowledge, like plumbing or baseball, but a combination of all other sets of knowledge, a discipline that can make use of all other disciplines.

Because metaphors are rooted in experience, we cannot invent them *ex nihilo* or consider them to be entirely arbitrary. Metaphor, like narrative, is not an imposition on historical experience, but an essential part of it. Metaphorical thinking does not tell us what is true, but it gives us a variety of ways to interpret a series of events. To make sense of the past, we need a multitude of metaphors which can help us approximate, but not reach complete precision or ultimate historical truth. We too often assume we also share conceptual metaphors, those which give shape to abstract meaning. But to understand how we interpret history, we also need to investigate the sources of knowledge and the types of metaphors we use to structure our frameworks of interpretation.

I have now made my case about metaphors in creative historical thinking. At this point, however, I must add the caveat that creativity in history is not a license to invent narratives simply to satisfy our political leanings, religious views, or ethical priors, without any regard for objective truth. Metaphors for history are not literal truths, but they express truths via comparisons. These metaphors can be incorrectly applied, of course, if they propose a relationship that, upon further investigation, turns out to be impossible. For this reason, I reject the idea, popular among postmodernists, that historical writing is the same as fiction, because this view denies the explanatory power of history, its rootedness in verifiable facts, and the correspondence of its investigations. Although historical knowledge can never be as certain as a logical proof, and though it is fallible, it is more than an invented narrative, a fictional construction, or a literary performance. History, unlike historical fiction, intends to be an accurate picture of the past. Although all history is an attempt to make sense of the evidence of the past from a particular point of view, what historians write and say are argued opinions, not ultimate truths. There is, in the words of the historian Herbert Muller, "no 'pure history,' history-in-itself from nobody's point of view, for nobody's sake."[14]

A history book then, is not a book of truths, but a book of perspectives argued faithfully from sources, interpreted through the unique lenses of its writer or writers. On this point, I hope that the pages to follow reflect the wisdom of the German polymath, Wilhelm von Humbolt, who wrote that a historian is creative like a poet, but "subordinates his imagination to experience and the investigation of reality."[15]

Written history is more than a list of literal facts—it is an attempt to communicate abstract thought. More precisely, it is the working out of our individual experiences shaped by collective metaphors and intended for social consumption. There will always be disagreements about how to interpret evidence, but by recognizing that history is a creative discipline, and by trying to understand the ways others see the past, we can better explore and communicate our own views on history. So, when you find something that you think is a shovel, take a second to think if there might be another possible interpretation. Maybe that shovel is a hat. And when someone else tells you that what you think is a shovel or a hat is actually a canoe paddle, consider if that possibility might also be true. An attitude of openness, curiosity, and play is essential for creative historical thinking.

thesis for my course

Notes

1. With a bit of kidding, I like to deny the 1066 Norman invasion of England by saying that it might have happened in 1065 for all I know, but we lost track along the way.
2. Robert Nisbet, *Social Change and History: Aspects of Western Theory of Development* (New York: Oxford University Press, 1969), 4.
3. George Lakoff and Mark Johnson, *Metaphors We Live By* (Chicago: University of Chicago Press, 1980); George Lakoff and Mark Johnson, *Philosophy in the Flesh: The Embodied Mind and Its Challenge to Western Thought* (New York: Basic Books, 1999).
4. Raymond W. Gibbs, *Embodiment and Cognitive Science* (Cambridge: Cambridge University Press, 2006), 9.
5. I'd like to thank coffee for the important role it played in the creation of this book.
6. Lakoff and Johnson, *Philosophy in the Flesh*, 47.
7. David Bayne Horn, *Frederick the Great and the Rise of Prussia* (London: English Universities Press, 1964).
8. John Harold Plumb, *Death of the Past* (London: Pelican Books, 1973 [original 1969]), 82.
9. Arthur Koestler, *The Act of Creation* (New York: Macmillan, 1964), 35.
10. Koestler, *The Act of Creation*, 119–120.
11. Creativity researcher Mihaly Csikzentmihalyi notes that each of these frames of reference or domains has "its own symbolic elements, its own rules, and generally has its own system of notation." The mixing of domains has also been labeled "conceptual blending," which Giles Fauconnier and Mark Turner insist is "a general, basic mental operation" that is "ubiquitous in everyday thought and language." Mihaly Csikzentmihalyi, *Creativity: The Psychology of Discovery and Invention*

(New York: Harper Perennial, 2013 [original 1997]), 37; Giles Fauconnier and Mark Turner, *The Way We Think: Conceptual Blending and the Mind's Hidden Complexities* (New York: Basic Books, 2003), 37.

12. Dedre Genter and Phillip Wolff, "Metaphor and Knowledge Change" in E. Dietrich and A. Markman, eds. *Cognitive Dynamics: Conceptual Change in Humans and Machines* (Mahwah, NJ: Lawrence Erlbaum Associates, 2000), 295–342.

13. Douglas Hofstadter, *Godel, Escher, Bach: An Eternal Golden Braid: A Metaphorical Fugue on Minds and Machines in the Spirit of Lewis Carroll* (New York: Vintage, 1979), 49.

14. Herbert J. Muller, *The Uses of the Past, Profiles of Former Societies* (Oxford: Oxford University Press, 1957), 43.

15. Wilhelm von Humboldt, "On the Historian's Task" *History and Theory* 6:1 (1967), 57–71, specifically 58. Translation of the German original *Über die Aufgabe des Geschichtschreibers* (1821).

Section I

The Argument

Seeing History as a Creative Discipline

Forecasts argument in chapters 1, 2, & 3

Section I offers suggestions for how to think of history as a creative discipline. This section consists of three chapters. Chapter 1 presents various images of how we might think of time in terms of space. It argues that we must create some kind of organizational system for time in order to make sense of the past, but that each of us has our own particular way of doing so. Basic metaphors of space and time provide us with frameworks for interpreting the past. Building on this point, Chapter 2 explores alternative visions of history that do not rely solely on two-dimensional linear timelines. Chapter 3 argues that imaginative ability—not the acquisition and recall of facts—is at the core of thinking like an historian and ought to be promoted in history classrooms.

1. How do we envision/imagine time & space? (Gets @ our organizational system, or organizing metaphor) How do we explain the experience of past peoples who didn't believe that human society changed over time?

2. How can we envision history as something other than a 2D timeline?

3. Historical thinking is fed by imagination & not by gathering & recalling facts.

1   Metaphors of Space and Time

At work at the Los Alamos National Laboratory in the early 1940s, the physicist Richard Feynman would frequently be found playing games, making practical jokes, or otherwise challenging the typically somber nature of scientific work. One day, Feynman began to test his own ability to count accurately to a minute. He noticed that when he counted to sixty seconds in his mind and only afterwards looked to a clock, he was always a few seconds short of a true minute. So he calibrated his mental clock, and when he had counted to fifty-two, he knew by repeated trial and error that roughly a minute had passed. Feynman then demonstrated to others that he could count quite accurately to a minute while engaged in just about any other task, as long as he wasn't in a conversation. Feynman's colleague, John Tukey, found that he could quite easily count to sixty while talking to others, but Tukey found it difficult to replicate the combination of manual tasks and counting that Feynman could accomplish so easily. Upon further investigation, Feynman and Tukey discovered that they were using different methods to count to a minute. Feynman used a verbal sense and "heard" the numbers being called, whereas Tukey counted time by "watching" a second-hand on an imagined mental clock. The discovery called into question the two scientists' most basic assumptions. "And so it struck me," Feynman recalled,

> "If that's already true at the most elementary level . . . that the imagery and method by which we are storing it all, and how we think about it, could be really . . . entirely different, and in fact, why somebody sometimes has a great deal of difficulty understanding a point which you see as obvious, and vice-versa, it may be because it is a little hard to translate what you just said into his particular framework and so on."[1]

This story raises an interesting question about how we understand and experience historical time. Nearly everyone has wondered whether what one person sees as red or green is the same red or green that another person sees. But few of us, I suppose, have questioned our basic assumptions about how we experience time. What if we all process and imagine time in different ways?

I encountered this issue firsthand when I once described to others how I visualize the calendar year. When I think about the calendar, I automatically, even reflexively, envision a circle with the summer months on top, autumn to the right like the east end of a compass rose, the winter months on the bottom of the circle, and spring months on the left. In my mind, the year is a circle, with the present moment progressing around it in a clockwise manner. It may be that I saw an image like this when I was young. My twin brother also "sees" or imagines the calendar the same way. But if you ask around, you might find that it is more common for people to imagine the calendar with summer at the bottom of a circle. Some, however, naturally view the months in vertical form, or think of the year passing like a flip calendar or a birthday calendar, each month being removed to reveal the next. Then again, many people claim not to view the year in spatial form at all.

Let's try a simple experiment to investigate this thought further. When I ask you to visualize the days of the week, for example, what do you see? Can you draw it? Is Sunday the first day, on the left, with the rest of the days of the week unfolding to the right, with Saturday at the far end? Or is Sunday at the right end of your list? Maybe you do not see the days of the week in a form from left to right at all. Maybe, for you, the week descends vertically from Sunday at the top of the list, or perhaps the days of the week form a circle.[2]

Social conventions and our own experiences affect whether we see Sunday or Monday as the first day of the week, and whether we see the year beginning with the opening of school in September instead of with the New Year on January 1. As an academic, my year begins in September. My father, an accountant, thinks in terms of a fiscal year instead. I imagine the switch from analog to digital clocks led to a general societal reconceptualization of time. Time used to flow "clockwise," as sure as the day is long. But will children always learn to tell time this way? Time will tell. Perhaps the main conception of time will be "Facebook time," with its upward flowing direction: new events at the top, older events down below.

In my history classes, I have asked students to draw the day, the week, and the month in whatever spatial arrangement they find most natural and satisfying (Figure 1.1). Obviously, there is some basic overlap of categories in how we visualize time, without which we would be unable to coordinate schedules or share social understanding of time. Tools such as traditional calendars, clocks, and reporting schedules provide us with objective standards of time, but our minds can mold these standards into subjective representations that are useful for our own purposes.[3] Clocks and calendars, in particular, began as useful metaphors of the motions of the sun and moon, while the term "period" (as in the somewhat redundant "period of time") comes from the Greek word for circular path. Over time, we forget the metaphorical link between the two concrete objects.

To draw your own perceptions of time, you must be open and honest about sketching time as you see it and not as how you imagine others want you to see it. There is no right or wrong way to look at time, although some visualizations

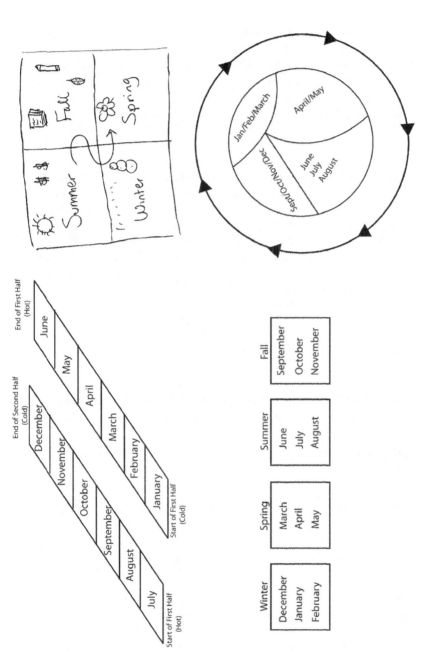

Figure 1.1 Mental Views of the Year

These are just some of the many examples of spatial representations of the year that college students in my courses have drawn.

may be more effective than others at storing or sorting information. The year as a circle is a common perception. Winter may be found on any side, and time may pass in a clockwise or counter-clockwise path.[4] In visualizing the year, we may break it up into all kinds of patterns. Historically, different people have broken the year into from two to eight seasons, eleven to thirteen months, or various other periods. Most calendars have been lunar or solar calendars—that is, based on the relative positions of the sun and moon—or a combination of the two. We have added leap years, leap days, hours, minutes, and seconds to recalibrate time. We have moved entire countries to new calendar systems, such as the transition from the Julian to the Gregorian calendar. Apparently, in the first decades of the eighteenth century, Sweden transitioned from the Julian to the Gregorian calendar over a period of forty years by skipping leap days until the 12-day difference between the two calendars was reconciled. This must create a massive headache for historians working on this period of Swedish history.[5] Even within a society that agrees on a periodization of time, there are individual differences in how one might represent time's structure (Figure 1.2). A schema that may seem reasonable to one person may appear incorrect or frustrating to another. Forcing learners to work within one framework is a major source of frustration, even if it is efficient for bureaucracy.

In our attempts to draw perceptions of time, it seems that we cannot get around the fact that humans conceive of time through spatial metaphors. When we say that time "flows like a river" or "flies like an arrow," our metaphors are based on distance, a property we know experientially, without abstraction. Because time is so difficult to get our hands on, we lean towards poetic descriptions. "Time, she's a fast old train" and "how soft time flies past your window at night," sings Townes Van Zandt. When we say that history has a direction, that it moves in a line, or is cyclical, we are also using spatial metaphors. We even

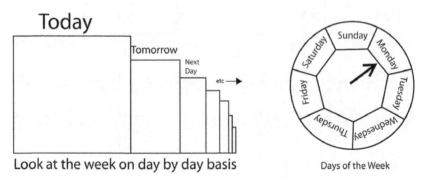

Look at the week on day by day basis   Days of the Week

Figure 1.2 Mental Views of the Week

One person's perception of the week differs from another's. We might imagine important days or slow days to be larger in our mental representation. The week may proceed in a line, or, as in this example, a circle, with an arrow pointing to the present day.

call time "the fourth dimension" as if it is of the same nature as the first, second, and third dimensions.

Although the process of thinking of time in terms of space is nearly universal, our spatial skills and particular spatial perceptions of time appear idiosyncratic. Lakoff and Johnson express the view that:

> The spatial metaphor for time seems to be an automatic part of our cognitive conscious that structures not only the way we conceptualize the relationship between events and time but the very way we experience time. That is why we necessarily think of events as occurring *at* times or *in* times.[6]

Scientists have also coined a technical term for imaging time in spatial form. They call it "spatial sequence synesthesia." According to neuroscientists Richard Cytowic and David Eagleman, synesthesia—or mixing of the senses—is "a hereditary condition in which a triggering stimulus evokes the automatic, involuntary, affect-laden, and conscious perception of a physical or conception property that's different from that of the trigger."[7] For some people, months have color, and for others, numbers may have shape. With mixed senses, numbers or colors can have taste, or certain sounds might correspond with certain colors. About 5 percent of the population carry the genes for synesthesia, but only 4 percent express automatic, involuntary sensory coupling. All of us, however, experience some overlap of the senses—we think loud is big, sharp tones are bright, and dark colors have strong flavors.

Spatial perception can overlap with a variety of other senses. Some people, I am told, see number lines, or imagine numbers taking up physical space on a particular path. They describe numbers climbing up stairs, or moving in progression from left to right as they count. A musician once told me that he sees the numbers 1, 3, 5, and 7 rising toward the upper right-hand corner of a page, and corresponding with the notes of a song. I cannot say that I see numbers the same way, but it does seem more natural to me when a chain of numbers is written rising from left to right: 1, 2, 3, 4, 5 rather than from right to left: 5, 4, 3, 2, 1.

From Mental Maps to Mental Timelines

In order to encourage others to think about how they might represent time in spatial form, it is helpful to draw a parallel between spatial representations of time and the concept of "mental maps" known to the field of cultural geography.[8] Mental maps are a form of mental representation—the ways we see the world. They are models with intended explanatory power. When you give directions to a visitor in your town, you are retrieving information from your mental map.

How we relate to geographical space varies from person to person. My mother, for example, gives directions around her home town using Catholic churches as points of reference; my father uses streets and compass directions. In technical terms, my mother uses network maps, and my father uses vector maps. In a conversation about how to get somewhere, they sound like they are speaking two separate languages.

How we conceive of the relationship between space and place relies to some extent on our experiences. In the United States, some of us think of going "back east" if we are from the East Coast originally, whereas those from the middle of the country are more likely to use the phrase "out east" to refer to the same thing. "Up north" has a fairly well-defined context in my home state of Michigan: it begins near the 44th parallel, where people go hunting over Thanksgiving break. Where "the South" begins is a contentious question in the United States, and is often resolved by reference to what states joined the Confederacy, the extent of the spread of the plant kudzu, the use of the third-person plural "y'all," or even the comical "IHOP–Waffle House line" referring to the geographical competition between two restaurant chains. In the Shenandoah Valley, the old timers still go "down" to the city of Winchester, following the river to the north. In Massachusetts, people speak of going "down" to Maine, via the ocean currents. In North Carolina, meanwhile, people go "down" in elevation to go east, towards the Atlantic coast. And believe it or not, Upper Canada is south of Lower Canada. No wonder the explorers couldn't find the Northwest Passage.[9] Likewise, the mysterious origin of the River Nile was to be found south, "up" the river.

I suppose everyone has at one time or another drawn a mental map, and it offers little conceptual difficulty. In my classes, I ask students to draw a map by hand, in just five minutes, showing their route to and from class. No two maps are ever entirely the same, of course, and none are to scale. Nevertheless, most of the maps are easily understood. This shows that while we all produce our own versions of spatial reality, we can see particular landmarks that communicate to all of us in a social community. Mental maps tend to highlight important parts of a route, with streets labeled to indicate where to turn. Such maps tend to include informal but understood cultural references. Where a professionally made street map might give you numbered addresses, a mental map is more likely to describe a route by referencing visible features like "a giant blue gorilla" outside a car dealership or "that old pink Victorian house."

We are motivated by similar concerns when we make maps or timelines from memory. Without reference to any outside source, try to draw a map of the United States. Go ahead. I'll wait.[10] Instead of aiming for cartographic precision, draw the map according to your personal knowledge of the geography and culture of the country. For instance, you may leave an entire region blank if you know nothing about it, or you might draw your home state larger and with greater accuracy than other states. Fill in the places that are important to you and your view of the world.

[Blank space here for drawing a mental map]

These kinds of visual representations demonstrate domains of knowledge but also reveal areas of ignorance (Figure 1.3). Students in Virginia, for example, often know next to nothing about the Midwest, and many students in Florida cannot tell you if Baltimore is north or south of Philadelphia. Native Texans might lump together the entire rest of the United States as "Not Texas." Europeans not accustomed to American geography might think they can just catch a bus from New York City to Detroit, without realizing that this is the mortal equivalent of an actual medieval ordeal. Creative doodles and labels for states demonstrate stereotypes, which are essentially convenient categories of summarizing complexity. Different kinds of maps serve different purposes. A good geographer knows that a highly detailed, precise map is not always the most useful, and that a simple map, even a distorted map, may be more convenient or appropriate for a particular purpose.

I have been speaking of literal maps, but now let's think about the idea of history as mapping. A friend of mine extends the analogy this way:

"mapping" history

> In my experience in history classes, teachers have been trying to get me to have the most accurate map [the most accurate view of the past] at the end of the course, which hasn't been particularly useful for my goals. Depending on the goal, different levels of abstractions may be more useful than others.

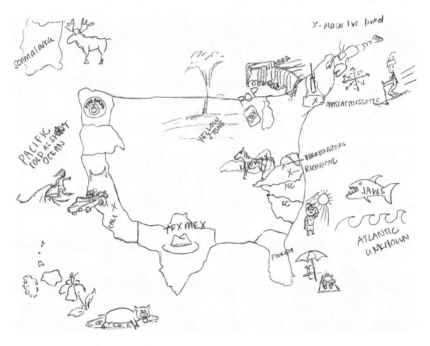

Figure 1.3 Mental Map of the United States

Knowledge of a location translates to precision in a mental map. Empty spaces suggest a lack of knowledge.

This friend has recognized that the goal of history is not singular. There is not one giant map, nor one comprehensive story historians are working on.[11] Instead, they are all approaching the past from different perspectives and for different reasons. Obviously, there can be good maps and bad maps. But the various kinds of maps—topological, political, hydrological, etc.—each serve their own purpose. Similarly, each historical explanation is useful for particular and limited ends.

Mental Timelines

Just as we all view the world differently when thinking of geography, time, or numbers, I think we all view the flow of history in individual ways, as well. Instead of a "mental map," let's call it a "mental timeline." For many people, a mental timeline consists mostly of events that occurred during their lives. Events that happened before they were born are often viewed as a different kind of history, something left mostly to the academic realm, with little bearing on the course of their lives. The events in our personal lives are not learned from textbooks. As children, we begin slowly (though seldom deliberately) to piece together the events of the past. Parents and grandparents, along with historical movies and television shows are the main sources of historical information for most people, and so naturally our surroundings and our culture affect how we understand history. Formal education begins to broaden the scope and deepen the details of a young person's awareness of history outside his or her own family and culture. When I was about 7 years old, my mental timeline was pretty simple, and looked something like Figure 1.4.

Our mental timelines are structures for the organization of our life stories, the scaffolding used to construct our understanding of time. These stories are constantly changing, as are our mental timelines. Not only do we add new events and new information to the story, but we also rearrange the sequence of events to build our autobiographical self and our individuality. The stories we tell ourselves about our lives help us to place our present selves on a mental timeline between a reconstructed past and an imagined future. We retell our life stories, with a focus on the main events so that we might find ways to explain our behavior, our identities, and our role in society. We might imagine our timelines crossing space, linking literal places. Place, for instance, may serve as a time marker. When historians say something like "Lindisfarne was not the only time the Vikings raided England," the place "Lindisfarne" stands for an event that can be plotted on a timeline. In our own timelines, places like "home," the location of a terrible accident, or a secret hideaway can play important structural roles.

Just as mental maps are inaccurate, not-to-scale versions of real printed maps, so also mental timelines are contorted, skewed, abbreviated versions of textbook historical timelines, with important events in starker relief. As with mental maps, mental timelines squeeze the distance between two points, and neglect unimportant points passed along the way. Mental timelines not only chart historical change, but they demonstrate a variety of phenomenon about how we view history. When people tell their own stories, those stories

Figure 1.4 Childhood Mental Timeline

My childhood mental timeline: Cave Man → Cloud of Smoke (symbolizing vague knowledge) → Revolutionary War soldier → Grandma (my actual Grandma, Ionia County Fair, Michigan, 1937). Image sketch credit to Xavier Mera.

are often extremely neat and tidy, whereas reality is messy. History is also messy and complicated, though when you read history textbooks, it seems so straightforward and uncomplicated. When people tell their own stories, it's not actually the whole truth and nothing but the truth. It's their own constructed narrative, with selected truths.

When I asked my students to make "mental timelines," I discovered that there is quite a variety of ways in which people view the flow of time. One student says he sees time like a measuring stick, progressing upwards so that the most recent events are on the top of the stick. There, the millimeters and centimeters, or the minutes and hours, are clearly defined, while lower on the stick, there are only feet and yards [I apologize for mixing units of measurement, but that is how the student defined it]. Another tells me she sees her life in five-year blocks, each in a different color. A third says he sees his timeline defined by blocks corresponding to ex-girlfriends, a statement which brought an eruption of laughter in the class.

When prompted to draw a mental timeline of their own lives, a lot of my students draw a line from left to right, which rises or falls depending on their perceived state of happiness. A rise indicates a good part of their life, and a descent stands for a negative event like a parental divorce or the loss of a family member or a pet. Most important events seem to be vacations, the birth of a brother or sister, and acceptance into college. Pain leaves it mark: dog bites, broken arms, broken hearts, and deaths in the family populate our mental timelines. Density of experience slows time and extends its spatial representation. Some see the past developing like the board game Candyland, with a winding path from their birth, laden with obstacles on the way to some final goal. Some people divide history into years based on where they lived, or what school they attended. These chunks of time are delineated by the very spaces where the time was spent. In general, for those who can or do imagine time in spatial form, the recent past occupies an inordinate amount of space.[12]

For most people, though, mental timelines do not consist of military and political facts—the standard fare of textbook history.[13] Instead, their timelines are populated by events in their own lives. In our mental timelines, we show little understanding about years and eras before we were born. Movies, not books (and certainly not textbooks), fill in the cultural highlights of the decades of previous generations. We are often guilty of presentism—the valuing of the recent events over the past—and it is true that, as a society we tend to value the recent past more highly than the distant past. In respect to this, mental timelines often reflect a logarithmic categorization of the past. So, the last ten years might be given as much space on a mental timeline as the hundred years before that, and the thousand years before that. In this way, we condense the distant past to make it fit more easily on a single scale. There is always a preference for recent facts, because we can remember these more easily. But otherwise, history is mostly a void. Our mental timelines, put on paper, indicate that we see the distant past as mostly irrelevant.

Goal = link individual mental timelines + academic history (Placing of self on the map of history.)

For too long, we have lamented the historical ignorance of the youth by thinking that "Because kids can't remember what I think they should remember, they must not remember anything at all." Unless an event can be seen to have an impact on your life, you are probably not going to remember it, and demanding the recall of unimportant historical facts is counterproductive to the study of history. There is good reason why I don't know who won the Ohio gubernatorial election of 1876: it seems like such a ridiculous thing to need to be told to know.[14] History must be interesting and relevant if we are to remember it. In the end, historical facts must be part of the history curriculum, but they need to be taught in context, and in ways that make sure their relevance is apparent. By recognizing the structures of our thinking about time, we help give relevance to historical facts, enable communication between people, and become open to new varieties of historical thinking.

Your personal mental timeline can be quite detailed, even if you have little understanding of academic history.[15] In fact, our mental timelines fit together with textbook narratives like square pegs in round holes. In the American context, middle- and high school-level courses usually introduce students to political and military events of national importance. Unable to see the relevance of academic history as taught in classrooms, many cast off history altogether as an irrelevant subject, as a story designed for other people, but not for themselves. Attempts to remedy this problem by bringing African American, Native American, and women's history into the classroom are well intentioned, but they do not necessarily bridge the gap between the textbook and lived experience. My own history education in primary school in the 1980s and 1990s was, as I recall, heavily invested in lessons on Ottawa Indians and the history of African American literature. This was a form of overcompensating for the nationalistic and often bigoted history curricula that dominated in earlier generations. Schools that take care to incorporate minority histories into the curriculum are right to do so, but merely representing more groups of people is not always enough to create meaningful connections between personal narrative and the broader map of academic history.

If we are to bridge the divide between our life stories and the histories we hear in the classroom, we need to re-think the nature of history as a discipline and introduce a diversity of ways of thinking about time and the relevance of the past. In traditional cultures, one or more persons in a community becomes a collector of stories, yet historical knowledge remains diffuse. In modern American culture, on the other hand, our communal, informal, and diffuse collective historical knowledge is largely absent from classroom history. We don't bring elders into the class to tell stories, but we should. We treat history as a formal set of knowledge contained in textbooks, and not as a living, evolving set of socially negotiated stories.

Some of us recover from the paradigms of academic history to seek historical knowledge in our own communities. We discover an interest in Civil War novels, Ancient Greece, genealogy, or our own ethnic history. We learn the importance of keeping a diary or a journal. Those who once rejected academic history then find something about history that appeals to them, something that compliments or reinforces their own mental timelines or geographies of being. It is this return to personal history that motivates us to try again to place ourselves on the map of history.[16]

Notes

1. Richard Feynman, "It's as Simple as One, Two, Three . . ." *Engineering & Science* 52:1 (Fall 1988), Cal Tech Library, accessed May 2, 2016.
2. Dutch calendars often have the days listed in a column on the left side of the page. The first day of the month is in the upper-left hand corner of the calendar, and the days follow first by descending down the page. The second week begins again at the top of the second column. In other words, the calendar is designed for eyes to travel first from top to bottom, then from left to right. Typical modern American calendars, by contrast, are designed so that days proceed first from left to right, and then from top to bottom.
3. Wanda J. Orlikowski and JoAnne Yates, "It's About Time: Temporal Structuring in Organizations" *Organization Science* 13:6 (2002), 684–700.
4. When I write that winter may be found on any "side" of the circle, I unconsciously display my idiosyncratic view again. My friend, Lydia Ingram, asks "Do circles really have sides, though?" This is quite the philosophical question. Mathematicians can tell you that, technically, it is impossible to "square the circle." My imagined circle of the year has four imagined sides: up, right, down, and left, in that order.
5. Perhaps some enterprising Swedish historian has already created a handy eighteenth-century Swedish Julian to Gregorian translation chart.
6. George Lakoff and Mark Johnson, *Philosophy in the Flesh: The Embodied Mind and Its Challenge to Western Thought* (New York: Basic Books, 1999), 153. Emphasis in original.
7. Richard E. Cytowic and David M. Eagleman, *Wednesday Is Indigo Blue: Discovering the Brain of Synesthesia* (Cambridge, MA: MIT Press, 2009), 112. See also Richard E. Cytowic, *Synesthesia: A Union of the Senses* (Cambridge, MA: MIT Press, 2002 [original Boston, MA: Springer Verlag, 1989]).
8. Some of the best work on mental maps comes from Yi-Fu Tuan. For more information about the relationship between mental maps and concepts of time, see chapter nine "Time in Experiential Space" in Yi-Fu Tuan, *Space and Place: The Perspective of Experience* (Minneapolis: University of Minnesota Press, 1977).
9. The history of Canada, sometimes called "beaver and railroad history," is a long story of how, for three and a half centuries, people tried to get around Canada but failed.
10. I'm not actually waiting, so what difference does it make to me how long you take?
11. I've encountered historians who seem to think that all histories—whether they be local, familial, or thematic—must somehow also contribute to a single, larger History with a capital H. I tend to think of each history as an independent, perspectival answer for a particular problem, not just a piece in a larger historical puzzle.
12. This agrees with a much earlier study that demonstrated wide variety in student drawings of time. Joy Paul Guilford, "Spatial Symbols in the Apprehension of Time" *The American Journal of Psychology* 37:3 (July, 1926), 420–423.
13. Military history, also known by the moniker "drum and bugle" history or "fife and drum" history, is perhaps the oldest form of history writing. It was from the outset political history, but is less so today.

14. As one reader pointed out, there was no gubernatorial election in Ohio 1876. Rutherford B. Hayes was elected governor of Ohio in 1875 and served until 1877. I cannot imagine how my life can be improved by this knowledge.
15. Dan P. McAdams, "Personal Narratives and the Life Story" in Oliver P. John, Richard W. Robins, and Lawrence A. Pervin, eds. *Handbook of Personality: Theory and Research*, 3rd edition (New York: Wilford Press, 2008), 242–263.
16. Roy Rosenzweig and David Thelen, *The Presence of the Past: Popular Uses of History in American Life* (New York: Columbia University Press, 1998).

2　Beyond Simple Linear History

I can use the example of Smoots!

Now that we have explored some of the ways in which people visualize time in spatial form and how they shape mental timelines to match their lived experiences, we can investigate a variety of ways historians might use timelines to tell their stories.

Historians, I believe, have too often assumed that we all see the world in the same way, that varieties of perception lie on a spectrum from poor to excellent, or from undeveloped to developed. At the poor end of the scale, we might speak of people who can distinguish historical time only in the roughest sense, and who use general terms like "back then" or "in the olden days." Those with a developed view of history can make fine distinctions between historical periods. The historian Carl Gustavson even believed that a sign of a grown-up mind was the ability to see time clearly as a linear progression from left to right. He wrote:

> A profound development of the sense of time occurs at about the age of ten or eleven. The child now has the advantage of more personal perspective. He still finds it difficult to visualize long duration in history, but he can see *points* of time, definite dates when things occurred, and he has become aware of events happening before and after a given point. . . . Apparently the most usual means whereby time is visualized is by the application of the knowledge of space. That is, the person has learned to measure nearness to himself of observed objects; he is now doing the same with time. Events of history are visualized in a linear manner, a straight line with events strung out upon it in chronological order.[1]

The tendency is for historians like Gustavson to think of historical-mindedness and time-metaphors as a matter of common sense. For many, history is a non-theoretical discipline; it is nothing but applied common sense. The historian Bernard Norling, for example, wrote: "The study of history is merely the application of this common sense principle to a broader field."[2]

This is an old view, and Norling was obviously not alone in holding it. The historian John Martin Vincent, in a history methods book from 1929, said nearly the same thing when he wrote that "the use of historical evidence is not a mysterious operation. it is only the constructive application of common sense to the data which the investigator has accumulated."[3] Another historian equates common sense with general knowledge and writes: "Historical explanation . . . obviously has affinities with explanation in ordinary life."[4] According to John Lukacs, Jacob Burckhardt declared that history has no method—historians just need to know how to read.[5] An acquaintance of mine who is a best-selling author of history books has told me he thinks historians have no special skills—that what they do, anyone could do.

In light of all this, I prefer the words of Stephen Davies, a historian who counters with the rebuke that "when ideas are unquestioned and taken for granted, they remain inarticulate, existing only in the realm of 'common sense.'"[6] Similarly, the French historian Marc Bloch adds the wisdom that "common sense usually turns out to be nothing more than a compound of irrational postulates and hastily generalized experiences."[7] Everyone has probably been guilty of sometimes treating their own perspective as the common-sense view. Yet, two people with two "common-sense views" can disagree. Time is a fundamental concept for history, yet our concepts of time, and how we structure time, are not common. Because concepts of time underlie every historical narrative, studying the frameworks for how we understand time is a prerequisite for understanding how people view history. A relevant insight here comes from the German historical research field known as *Begriffsgeschichte*, or conceptual history. If we want to understand the past, they say, we must first understand how people in different ages envisioned history and the flow of time. Understanding that medieval people did not believe in social progress, for example, is crucial to not read people of that era with a presentist, progressive mindset. A leading thinker in this school, Reinhart Koselleck, believed that the modern world was defined by the awareness that we are part of history. Historicity, he wrote, is the sense that the human world changes over time.[8]

Our relationship with time changes quickly in the modern world. Two centuries ago, we could measure distance by the number of days it would take to sail somewhere or to get someplace on horseback. Railroads and telegraphs caused a revolution in our relationship to time. In the late nineteenth century, technology seemed to condense time and eliminate distances, inspiring stream-of-consciousness writing, Cubism, and Einstein's Theory of Relativity, which posited that there was no universal clock, but various times relative to the observer.[9] We then entered a new age of time perception. Although we generally measure time in consistent units of seconds, minutes, hours, days, and years, we also understand a variety of relative measurements of time like "a blink of an eye," "a mileway"—roughly the amount of time it takes to walk a minute—and "dog years." When the world's oldest person died at 117 years of age, a newspaper article described her life as lasting ninety Italian governments. I like the idea of an Italian government as a measurement of time, even if only for the comedic effect, since that length is notoriously unreliable.[10]

Today, our views of time continue to evolve. Psychologists and scholars of organizational management have probably produced the best works on how we experience time in the postmodern world. These groups have invented words like "polychronicity" to describe how we can manage multiple process flows at the same time, and "pluritemporalism" for our ability to structure time in multiple ways at once, with overlapping periodizations.[11] An undergraduate student who read an early draft of this book explained that her greatest struggle in middle school history classes was trying to understand that there were different sets of events happening simultaneously in multiple places on the globe. In her mind, there was just one timeline of all events. But this image was a product of how she had been taught. "I could not comprehend that New World happenings could go on at the same time as Old World happenings, because they were always taught as separate time periods," she wrote. We must realize that multiple story lines are always happening at the same time, and that historical narratives are always overlapping, particular, and incomplete.

In our minds, then, time is a malleable substance. We can chop it up, bend it, stretch it, or condense it. This leaves us with something of paradox. We think that time passes at the same rate for everyone (Einstein's theory aside), and yet we experience and relate to time in different ways. What then is history without a consistent understanding of time? In this chapter, I argue that while we can and should imagine time in different ways, we are also capable of understanding each other's views of time so long as we can intuit similar basic spatial metaphors. On this point, the social anthropologist Alfred Gell explains that:

> We have no dedicated sense-organ for the measurement of elapsed time, as we have for the measurement of vibrations in the air (forming sounds) or the wavelengths and relative positions of light-waves striking the retinas of our eyes. To speak of the "perceptions" of time is already to speak metaphorically.[12]

Others agree with Gell that we require minimal common measurements of time to coordinate social activities. Eviator Zerubavel, for example, proposes that there is a structural system that shapes collective memory. The ways we stretch, condense, and chop up time, he argues, are the results of socialization. While it may feel that we create these images of time in our mind, it could be possible that metaphors of lines, zigzags, cycles, trees, ladders, mountains and valleys, and others, are passed down through generations and reinforced socially through mnemonic devices.[13] Perhaps the way we view time in spatial form is even biologically determined. Rene Thom, one of the founders of chaos theory, anticipated Zerubavel's structural approach by seeking the root elements of biological systems. Thom speculated that every animal brain is equipped with a dynamic set of innate genetic forms (based on mathematical principles) that combine and morph to form local charts for motor or psychological activity. In play, we set up a system of rules within which we can experiment with mixing and combining these forms into new models, most of which are worthless and easily discarded. Following Thom, we might propose that our minds have a limited set of potential archetypes for dealing with spatial forms. Woven together, these forms can be put to use in forming representations of time. A line coming to a dead end, like a horizontal "T" represents ending; a line rising from the ground represents "emitting"; a line that comes to a "T" and ends, but then starts anew on the other side of the intersection, might represent change. Through these basic metaphors, we can read each other's maps of time. Over time, however, we learn through play to construct useful models for dealing with reality.[14]

Perhaps this is all a bit too complicated, and we don't need to understand the ultimate nature of time or the reason why we all view it in different ways to recognize just how important these differences are. Simply recognizing this diversity of viewpoints is an important first step towards accepting creative history because it teaches us that we can overcome some fundamental disagreements simply by understanding differences of perception. Yet, we are stuck with the problem that despite all of the ways in which we could imagine time and present history, our classrooms tend to promote just one view of historical time. In the West, the dominant view is that history should be represented by a timeline arrow going from left to right. Although I have little evidence, I suspect that the left-to-right orientation is a psychological manifestation of right-handedness (and with it, the tendency to write script with a pen or stylus from left to right) and might be related to our tendency to turn gradually right in a blizzard white-out, or to our propensity to first turn right when entering a building like a shopping mall. Perhaps our perceptions of time reflect genetic and biological principles at work.

At any rate, conventional history classes teach History with a capital H as an official kind of thing, existing along a single timeline, and consisting of an essential set of facts about certain important people and places. In this view, George Washington is part of History, and so is Abraham Lincoln, Michael Jackson, and Martin Luther King Jr., but not, say, your cousin, the grocery store clerk, or the guy down the street. If a teacher says "Choose a historical figure for your report," the implicit assumption is that you will not choose someone you know personally. People talk about "making" History when someone performs an important act like setting a sporting record. We are also prone to measure the amount of History that a place has, so that we can say that there is more History in Boston than in Boise, or more in Rome than in New York City.[15] This idea that some people are part of history and others are not—or that history is a quality which can be measured—betrays a conventional understanding of history that I like to call Simple Linear History. Simple Linear History is a mental concept that is a reflection of textbook timelines which show the past as a single trajectory with major people and events on it, listed in chronological order.

Simple Linear History is a kind of easy shortcut to make sense of the past. But it is also uncreative, limited, limiting, and potentially misleading. The view that history is just "one damn thing after another" contributes to the assumption of progress, and to the idea that there is only one overarching story to tell. It forces the chaos of the past into rigid periodization and misses all of the concurrence and overlapping rhythms that make that past so interesting. Without a doubt, most people feel alienated from the standard presentations of history. History for them exists as an academic subject in the classroom, but has little effect on their real lives. Simple Linear History is limiting, because people do not always experience or remember events in the chronological order in which they actually occurred. Certainly, we do not make sense of the large themes of history in real time, as they unfold.

Traditional Timelines in the Classroom

The results of the fact-based learning that goes along with Simple Linear History appear pretty dismal if we are to consider the ability of students to recall dates or to put major historical events in proper chronological order. I discovered this firsthand when I quizzed my own students. On the first day of class in a sophomore-level college course on U.S. history, I asked my students to each create a timeline with the following events dated and placed in chronological order: the ratification of the U.S. Constitution, the Wright Brothers' first flight, JFK's election, the fall of the Berlin Wall, the fall of the Soviet Union, the U.S. Civil War, World War I, the moon landing,[16] and World War II. All of these are basic history textbook facts. Here is one student's answer (Figure 2.1).

In the timeline shown in Figure 2.1, the student has confused the ratification of the Constitution with the signing of the Declaration of Independence, a very common mistake. It would be charitable to call "1786" a guess for the correct date of the Civil War, and the Wright Brothers here take to the skies before the world's first railroad has been built. But the student has a slightly better mental picture of the twentieth century. At least he manages to place the world wars in the correct decades, and he correctly dates the election of JFK (actually 1959) and the moon landing (actually 1969). It is fascinating to see, however, that younger generations cannot commonly identify the major events of only a single generation ago, events such as the fall of the Berlin Wall (1989) and the fall of the Soviet Union (1991). I suspect that in another generation from now, students will think that New York City's twin towers fell on September of 2011, hence the term 9/11.

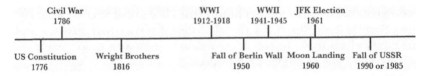

Figure 2.1 Student Timeline

Many students are terrible at placing dates on traditional timelines. But don't worry too much about it. It takes time and skill to visualize the past.

Now, you might accuse me of having chosen an outlier—the worst timeline in a large class of students—so that I might moralize about the ignorance of the youth. But the student timeline presented here represents a median result in the class. That is, I have not reproduced the best, most historically accurate timeline, nor have I chosen the worst example. In fact, this average timeline came from a student who appears, for all intents and purposes, to be quite intelligent. Not only has he navigated his way through a K–12 system and earned admission at one of the better universities in the state of Virginia, but he also demonstrated many admirable skills and, in my experience, appears to be a quick learner. And yet, the median student's historical ignorance is deep and wide. Certainly, without preparation, he would struggle to pass an eighth-grade history exam.

After this exercise, one student wrote "I apologize to every history teacher I ever had, and my dad." Another wrote "I was soooo wrong. . . . like not even close. I only got World War II. *sigh*" But to chide or ridicule these students for their historical ignorance is to miss the point. Unless you are a biologist, you've probably forgotten all about the Krebs Cycle, even though you spent a month on it in high school biology class. Facts once learned, but never applied, tend not to stick. If students feel that they must learn historical facts to appease other people or to meet social pressures, they won't be motivated to learn these facts for themselves. I am not pessimistic at all about the historical ignorance of the mass of the public. Considering the useless information they were probably supposed to have learned in high school, it is actually creditable that so many resisted.

Perhaps each generation is getting worse at connecting to history because the traditional textbooks events of history have become increasingly removed from our perceptions of time. When cultural change is slow, the past seems close at hand because it has more relevance and more to teach. When changes come quickly, time seems to speed up, traditions are broken, and there is more mental distance between the present and the past. Once upon a time, it might have mattered who your great-great-grandfather was or what ancestral claim was yours, but today our personal connection with the past is less important than ever. We live for the moment, and for the future, the past be damned.

I propose then that today's historical illiteracy is not necessarily a sign of the corruption of the youth. It may instead be a form of what economists call "rational ignorance." People always remember the history that matters and is useful to them, but it is rational for them to resist learning or forget history that has no bearing on their lives. For most people, useful, memorable history consists of events that happened during their own lives and which were experienced personally. So, someone in their fifties or sixties today might be more capable of accurately lining up the main events of the twentieth century, not because they came from a better, more attentive generation of students, but because these events happened within their lifetimes. Lived events leave a stronger imprint than learned events. Young people are not bad at history per se, but their historical knowledge never satisfies older generations. Each generation remembers its own history, fails to learn that of its parents, and then turns around to blame the next generation for repeating this pattern.

Stories That Move Backwards and Forwards

If we reject the model of Simple Linear History and reimagine history as a creative, inspiring discipline, we must be honest about how we actually relate to the past and how we experience the passing of time. The truth is, we do not always relate well to history in a linear sense. We never can learn history from beginning to end. Rather, we must start somewhere in the middle. I once explained to a British historian that I taught my survey course through chronologically overlapping thematic lessons, rather than marching through events one after another in a strictly chronological fashion. "Bonkers!" he declared.[17] The idea that a professor could teach thematic history to freshmen was, in his mind, inconceivable; it could not be done.

My British critic was not wholly wrong; there are some problems with history lessons organized by themes rather than by chronology. But these problems, I believe, are less worrisome than the problems of a straightforward narrative in which one only presents events in directly chronological order. I believe he was engaging in what the historian David Hackett Fischer has called "the chronic fallacy." Fischer defines this as "a kind of misplaced temporal literalism in which a historian forces his story into an over-rigid chronological sequence and tells everything in the precise order of its occurrence, with results that are dysfunctional to his explanatory purpose."[18] Ideally, a story progresses in chronological order, but such an order is not always possible or best if the story's goal is explanation (Figure 2.2).

No good story is ever directly linear, and attempts at linearity can potentially be a straightjacket for creative historians. Let me explain what I mean with an example from a class lecture, Figure 2.2 labeled "Non-linear Course of a Lecture." This figure shows the course of a lecture on the Great Depression. Dark arrows represent the material of the lecture, while dotted lines represent backtracking or jumping ahead in time to explain key events relative to other events.

In a lecture on the Great Depression, a professor references the following dates in such an order: 1929, 1921, 1913, 1929, 1936, and the 1960s. Now, from the perspective of an outsider, this arrangement may seem nonsensical. Why has our professor jumped around so much? How can someone be expected to follow the story? From the professor's perspective, however, this order probably makes perfect sense. First, she defines 1929 as the crucial moment of the stock market's crash. But to note that this wasn't the first crash in American history, she references an earlier depression in 1921. Perhaps to explain the rise of banking issues that lead to the Great Depression, she moves backwards again to 1913 to explain the development of the Federal Reserve. Then, forward to 1929 she goes, explaining how everything came together in one final catastrophe. From there, the story progresses through the years of

Non-Linear Course of a Course

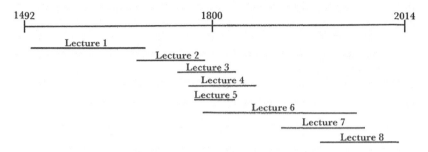

Non-Linear Course of a Lecture

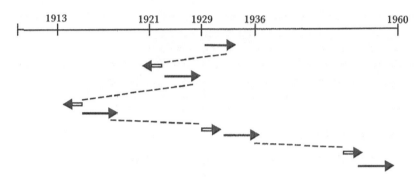

Figure 2.2 Non-Linear Course of a Source

This represents how a series of lectures on various themes might overlap chronologically. One lecture might not start precisely where the last one ended. Themes in history are necessarily overlapping, and sometimes it is necessary to reinforce a lesson by making a reference to another event or process at a different location on the timeline.

the Depression, and she specifically mentions 1936, a year when the Depression was at its deepest. At the end of the lecture, she may reference Keynesian economics and stagflation, thereby foreshadowing future lectures.

It would be possible for a chronicler to tell the history of the Great Depression by starting in 1929, never turning her head once, and only plowing straight ahead to 1940 or 1945 or whenever she thinks the logical end of the Great Depression may be. Lecturing without jumping around means that everything would have to be explained perfectly the first time through, and it assumes that the connections from this first event to the next were clear. The goal of storytelling is to explain cause and effect, how and why something went from A to B. But it is important to also understand that the shortest way to explain the distance between points A and B is usually not a straight line.

The next time you sit in on a history lecture, listen for each and every reference to a particular date, and then write these dates down, being careful to place them in the order in which they were spoken. Now, what you will probably notice is that the dates do not fall directly in chronological order. In fact, it would be very difficult indeed to tell a story without ever going backward to preface a fact, or without going forward to explain where the story is going. Good lecturers will probably jump around to some extent, so that they can explain both chronology and context. Granted, "jumping around" in a lecture appears at first glance to only complicate and confuse things, but it is actually quite natural and necessary. This needs to be done judiciously, of course, because it can be easy to confuse an audience by jumping around in the chronology too much. One common lecturing error of this type is what I like to call "the argument by reference to future argument." This occurs when a lecturer introduces a new idea, doesn't define it (and may not be able to define it), but suggests that the idea will be explained in a future lecture. Like characters introduced in a novel, terms in a lecture need to be defined when they first appear. Balancing the progress of a narrative with the necessity of explanatory asides is a skill for lecturers to learn. But storytelling without flashbacks, backtracking, foreshadowing, diversions, or asides is very limiting. Storytelling in a straight line would be quite boring, and indeed quite unnatural.

History Out of Line

The best stories, I think, are never straight lines, and straight-line textbook history can actually be deceptive. In real life, the rise and fall of action creates suspense, while a diversion from the trodden path introduces new elements to an old plot line. The literary critic Edmund Wilson recognized this irregular pacing in the works of the French historian Jules Michelet, whom Wilson praised for taking us along the winding course of history, "panting and talking at top speed" sometimes in "elliptical and obscure" fashion. Michelet's narrative "hasn't the ideal symmetry of art" Wilson said, "because the facts of history won't permit it."[19] Creative historians like Michelet do not try to force a story to fit a timeline or a particular pattern. Rather, they invent new ways of reframing old stories.

Metaphorical language at use in literature shapes the way we think about narratives. We speak of a "narrative arc" of a story, for example, and we say the past is "behind" us and the future is "in front of" of us. We might imagine the present as a surface riding on an accumulated past. Or, we might label the distant past as the dim recesses of time. The novelist Thomas Mann begins his *Joseph and His Brothers* with the phrase "Very deep in the well of the past," as if history begins down below and comes up.[20] Our language biases us to think that we need to get a story "straight" for it to be correct, and that something which is "crooked" is wrong. Too often, though, we try to force the facts of history into a straight line, when the actual course of events is much more messy.

Novelists like Mark Twain, Laurence Sterne, and Kurt Vonnegut all employed unconventional non-linear timelines to express new ways of looking at narrative time. They demonstrated that timelines that diverge from a traditional left-to-right linear model offer us the ability to think creatively about our subject and encode additional information. They showed, furthermore, that in thinking about narrative form through spatial diagrams, we can reshape time and seek new ways to understand history.

Laurence Sterne's *The Life and Opinions of Tristam Shandy, Gentleman*, sometimes described as the first novel, presents a good example of how one might relate to time in a creative way (Figure 2.3). Sterne was aware that his story was not straightforward, but was rather intentionally roundabout, and he felt that he needed to explain his unconventional thought process. He said that the narrative digressions within the first five volumes of his novel could be represented by five separate lines, five stories, each with its own meandering path.

The drawing shown in Figure 2.3 is from the first edition of Sterne's novel, which I don't own, but would gladly receive as a free copy, if a generous reader would be inclined. In the text that accompanies the image, Sterne apologized for not moving directly from A to B, from the beginning to the end. It was necessary, he said, to digress, backtrack, sidetrack, and foreshadow, if he were to explain himself. For Sterne, and for all of us, the goal of narrative

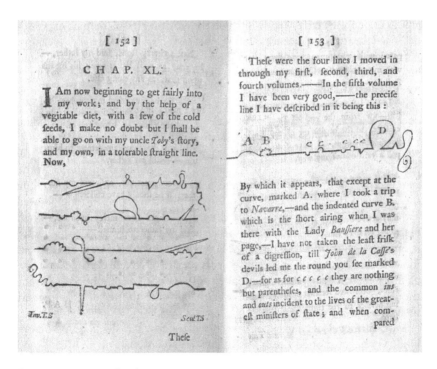

Figure 2.3 Tristram Shandy

Lawrence Sterne's visual description of his narrative line across four volumes of *The Life and Opinions of Tristam Shandy, Gentleman* (published in nine volumes from 1759–1767).

is eventually to get from the beginning to the end. But, how we get there is another story. Sterne put it this way:

> Could a historiographer drive on his history, as a muleteer drives on his mule,—straight forward;—for instance, from Rome all the way to Loretto, without ever once turning his head aside either to the right hand or to the left,—he might venture to foretell you an hour when he should get to his journey's end:—but the thing is, morally speaking, impossible; for, if he is a man of the least spirit, he will have fifty deviations from a straight line to make with this or that party as he goes along, which he can no ways avoid. He will have views and prospects to himself perpetually soliciting his eye, which he can no more help standing still to look at that he can fly.[21]

In fact, it seems to be the talent of the novelist to tell stories that are not straightforward. While historians like Hayden White propose that there are narrative structures that underlie and determine histories, the opposite seems to be the case in fictional stories that seek unconventional plot twists and turns. Not knowing where the story is ultimately headed can be as pleasurable as knowing exactly what will happen. Hermann Hesse's Demian expresses this need for irregular narrative form in his own life: "My story isn't pleasant, it's not sweet and harmonious like the invented stories; it tastes of folly and bewilderment, of madness and dream, like the life of all people who no longer want to lie to themselves."[22]

Creative timelines with non-linear structural features do more than introduce new ways to see the flow of time. They can also serve as mnemonic devices to aid memorization. Mark Twain—who, by the way, was known for seeing "South" as "up" on his mental map—taught audiences to imagine the past as a winding road, something similar to what children encounter in the game Candyland. For Twain, this was a memorization strategy for recalling the reigns of the British monarchs. Giving physical shape to time allowed Twain to more easily recall historical distance and progression. In an era when many lecturers on the public circuit read their speeches, Twain was famous for memorizing the entirety of his talks. Surviving pages from Twain's notebooks indicate that he outlined his lectures with a series of sketched images and diagrams, something similar to the modern concept of "sketchnoting" whereby the designer sets up a series of images that inspire the recall of important moments of a story.[23]

Kurt Vonnegut also imagined stories with shape, but shape of a different kind. Vonnegut plotted his narrative arcs on a Cartesian plane with x- and y- axes. He used the x-axis to represent time and the y-axis to represent mood. In a series of diagrams, he showed how he could represent the storyline, or arc of the story on a grid. His storyline arc went up and to the right if good fortune befell the main character, but it went down and to the right if the main character were struck by ill fortune. Time for Vonnegut always flowed from left to right on the page. But by charting another variable, good and bad fortune along the y-axis, Vonnegut discovered common shapes or archetypes for stories. Tragedies, for example, extended the line deep into the category of "ill fortune."

A mental timeline from a student in my U.S. history survey, shown here in Figure 2.4, demonstrates another way to add non-linear elements to a timeline. As an artist, the student responded well to my request to be honest about drawing her actual perception of the past. In her mind, the distant past does not exist, and the twentieth century emerges from nothingness. Movies like *Grease* inform her image of the decades of the mid-century. In this view, time flows first in a linear fashion from left to right, but then flows cyclically after 1990, her birth year. Time, in her perspective, is punctuated by important personal events such as the birth of a brother, moves from one state to another, a trip to Florence, the beginning of college. She also adds another dimension to the scale: the width of the timeline increases as it approaches the present. This, she explained, represents the relative influence of recent memories and her greater

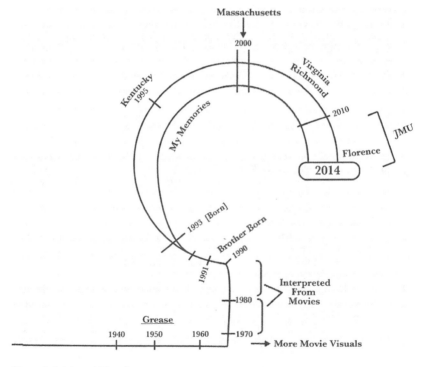

Figure 2.4 Mental Timelines

Mental timelines can demonstrate a vast amount of data in a short space. Adding non-linearity to a mental timeline contributes another variable of information. In this mental timeline, the mid-twentieth century is linear and without any labeled facts, but the lived past takes on a circular form, perhaps representing a closed or limited lifespan.

awareness of those newer memories over older memories. I am sympathetic to this diagram because of how it shows distinct breaks in knowledge about the past. When we venture into the light of the modern historical zone, time is full of meaning. But when we reach far enough into the past, we encounter darkness or a void, the end of a line.[24]

Creative spatial diagrams of time may be useful in this regard, because they inspire new ways of looking at the past, they aid in memorization, and they better reflect the diverse ways in which people look at and experience time. By recognizing social and indeed idiosyncratic perceptions of time, people are better able to respect the different views of others and help strengthen their understanding of how to translate historical perception. Spatial diagrams of time help us to consider creative alternatives to Simple Linear History.

Notes

1. Gustavson repeats this view in his book, *The Mansion of History* (New York: McGraw-Hill, 1976), 46.
2. Bernard Norling, *Towards a Better Understanding of History* (Notre Dame, IN: University of Notre Dame Press, 1960), 2.
3. John Martin Vincent, *Historical Research: An Outline of Theory and Practice* (New York: Peter Smith, 1929), 139. Also, on page iii, Vincent writes that "historical research is only the application of logic and common sense to the past affairs of mankind."
4. Trygve R. Tholfsen, *Historical Thinking* (New York: Harper & Row, 1967), 288.
5. John Lukacs, *The Future of History* (New Haven, CT: Yale University Press, 2011), 10–11.
6. Stephen Davies, *Empiricism in History* (New York: Palgrave, 2003), 1.
7. Marc Bloch, *The Historian's Craft* (New York: Alfred A. Knopf, 1963 [original 1953]), 80.
8. Reinhart Koselleck, *Futures Past: On the Semantics of Historical Time* (translated and with an introduction by Keith Tribe) (New York: Columbia University Press, 2004). Original English version, MIT Press, 1985; German original Frankfurt am Main: Suhrkamp Verlag, 1979.
9. Stephen Kern, *The Culture of Time and Space, 1880–1914* (Cambridge, MA: Harvard University Press, 1983).
10. I propose that "an Italian Government" becomes a slang form for a length of time. For an example of how to use it in a sentence: "I went to the DMW yesterday, and I just sat around waiting for what must have been, I dunno, six or seven Italian governments! It was miserable."
11. This scholarship points to an almost ubiquitous form of chronesthesia, or the ability to be aware of time outside of the present, a conscious awareness of subjective time also called mental time travel. Allen C. Bluedorn, *The Human Organization of Time: Temporal Realities and Experiences* (Stanford, CA: Stanford University Press, 2002); Endel Tulving, "Chronesthesia: Awareness of Subjective Time" in Donald T. Stuss and Robert C. Knight, eds., *Principles of Frontal Lobe Functions* (New York: Oxford University Press, 2002), 311–325; Marcelo Bucheli and Rohit Daniel Wadhwani, eds., *Organizations in Time: History, Theory, Methods* (Oxford: Oxford University Press, 2014); Helga Nowotny, "Time and Social Theory: Towards a Social Theory of Time" *Time & Society* 1:3 (1992), 421–454.
12. Alfred Gell, *The Anthropology of Time: Cultural Constructions of Temporal Maps and Images* (Oxford: Berg Publishers, 1992), 93.

13. Eviator Zerubavel, *Time Maps: Collective Memory and the Social Shape of the Past* (Chicago: The University of Chicago Press, 2003).
14. Rene Thom, *Structural Stability and Morphogenesis: An Outline of General Theory of Model* (Reading, MA: W.A. Benjamin, Inc., 1975 [French original from 1972]), 303–307; David Aubin, "Forms of Explanation in the Catastrophe Theory of Rene Thom: Topology, Morphogenesis, and Structuralism" in M.N. Wise, ed., *Growing Explanations: Historical Perspective on the Sciences of Complexity* (Durham, NC: Duke University Press, 2004), 95–130.
15. It seems to me that the amount of History a place has is roughly a function of: (the total amount of stuff that happen) × (the age of the stuff that happened) × (the political influence of this stuff that happened). In small towns, where a relatively small amount of stuff has happened, local historians lean on the third category, the political influence of this stuff (i.e. George Washington slept here, *Hier kotzte Goethe*) to make their claim for the town's importance.
16. Assuming that this actually happened! My apologies to the moon landing hoax conspiracy theorists.
17. Perhaps so, but I take humble comfort in what Alice said to the Mad Hatter in the Tim Burton movie remake of *Alice in Wonderland* "You're entirely bonkers. But I'll tell you a secret. All the best people are."
18. David Hackett Fischer, *Historians' Fallacies: Towards a Logic of Historical Thought* (New York: Harper & Row, 1970), 152.
19. Edmund Wilson, *To the Finland Station* (New York: Doubleday Anchor, 1953 [original 1940]), 14.
20. John W. Woods, translator. Thomas Mann, *Joseph and His Brothers: The Stories of Jacob, Young Joseph in Egypt, Joseph the Provider* (London: Everyman's Library, 2005, originally published in four volumes in Frankfurt am Main: S. Fischer Verlag, 1933–1943).
21. *The Work of Lawrence Sterne, Containing The Life and Opinions of Tristram Shandy, Gent., A Sentimental Journey Through France and Italy, Sermons, Letters, & c., with a life of the author written by himself* (London: George Routledge and Sons, 1849), 16.
22. Hermann Hesse, *Demian* (Mineloa, NY: Dover Publications, 2000 [original in German, Frankfurt am Main: S. Fischer Verlag, 1919]), 2.
23. Mark Twain, "How to Make History Dates Stick" *Harper's Monthly Magazine* (December 1914), 3–15. Twain's sketches themselves are viewable online, courtesy of the New York Public Library, "Notes in sketch form for a lecture. Inscribed to Charles [Warren Stoddart] at end of British lecture tour, 'January 9, 1874. 10.30pm.' *The New York Public Library Digital Collections*, https://digitalcollections.nypl.org/items/3edc6bc0-899d-0130-8be8-58d385a7b928, accessed March 21, 2018.
24. In general, I feel that there is a dark curtain somewhere in the past, located probably around the year 1910 in my mental timeline. This dark curtain separates what humanity knows through experience from what we know only through historical reconstruction. Historians can work on both sides of the curtain, but I prefer to work on the period before the curtain fell. Not only does this period seem more foreign, and therefore more curious to me, but I am comforted in my research by knowing that there is no one alive who can contradict me based on their personal experiences alone. Historians of the modern era have a greater burden in convincing others that they have gotten the story correct.

3 On Facts and Creative Interpretations

All of this talk of creativity in history, of drawings and imagination, is far removed from the fact-based learning we encounter in history classrooms. In the United States, the failure to learn the proper historical facts is seen not as just an intellectual failure but also a cultural or patriotic sin. If students perform poorly in math, they might be labeled as unintelligent. But if they perform poorly in history, they will be chided for being poorly informed citizens, or even bad people. There seems to be a transparent belief among some segments of society that good students fulfill civic, patriotic, and indeed moral duties by learning a core set of socially determined historical facts. A knowledge of these facts is said to be a remedy for all sorts of political and social problems, from voting for the wrong political party to investing in the wrong stocks. "Know your history," people say, generally meaning the facts of textbook history, "and you will not repeat the mistakes of the past." Aware of these empty proverbs, most of us find no positive, practical purpose for academic history. We only know that if we know certain historical facts we will be absolved from being judged delinquents. In America, we suffer through history class as a duty and a chore.

The fetishization of facts has long clouded the view of what a historian does. A lot of people think that history is just a collection of facts, and that the more facts you know, the more you know about history. Unfortunately, conventional wisdom sees the historian as a rather dull, lonely creature with an incredible memory and an insatiable appetite for facts. But, in truth, historians don't spend all day recording or recalling information about the past, as if preparing for a pub quiz trivia championship. They are not all white-haired men, and they don't dress only in tweed and corduroy. Novels and films abound with depictions of historians who fit the stereotype of the wise, old patriarch.[1]

For generations, historians have tried to remedy the image of their discipline. They have tried to explain that history is not a collection of facts, but a form of critical problem solving in which we seek evidence, weigh it, and give it meaning. In 1937, the historian Allen Nevis explained that:

> The true historical scholar is not the man who spills facts out of every pocket, who can tell instantly when Nicholas of Cusa lived and what

were the contents of the Constitutions of Clarendon—matters on which an encyclopedia can furnish more precise and interesting information. It is the man who, confronted with facts, assertions, and testimony offered with varying degrees of authority, knows how to test them, discard what seems false, and evaluate what seems true.[2]

A generation later, the historian E.H. Carr repeated this line of thought, ridiculing those who thought that history "consists of the compilation of a maximum number of irrefutable and objective facts." Carr wrote: "Anyone who succumbs to this heresy will either have to give up history as a bad job, and take to stamp-collecting or some other form of antiquarianism, or end up in the madhouse."[3]

Fortunately, in the past few decades, the "historical thinking" movement has encouraged a reorientation towards skills over content in history education. Most articles and books on historical thinking define it as a set of skills in source analysis, chronology, research, and writing, which need to be cultivated and taught in combination with historical facts. K–12 educators in particular have embraced the trend by designing lesson plans for interactive activities that inspire students to "do" history rather than just passively absorb its lessons.[4] According to Sam Wineburg, a leading figure in this discussion, historical thinking does not come naturally, but it can be learned if properly taught. Wineburg has taken a scientific approach to studying how students learn and think about history. He demonstrates empirically that most students are unable to draw relevant historical information from a text, and that they lack the ability to situate sources in their proper historical environment.[5] Facts without a framework or ability to interpret them are meaningless and potentially dangerous.

History is not a puzzle that can be completed, or a single story with a beginning and an end. All of the historians in the world, working together, will never produce a final textbook. They can never record everything or create some final, incontrovertible, unalterable product. This does not mean, however, that we ought to despair, or that we ought not to engage in historical research. Everyone thinks about the past now and then, and everyone is their own historian. R.G. Collingwood put this best when he wrote: "There are already as many historians as there are human beings, and the question is not Shall I be an historian or not? but How good an historian shall I be?"[6]

It is this broad sense of the term historian that we should promote. There are many people who do some history, and things that look like historical thinking, even when they are not history teachers or writers. First, there are groups of people who are not creating new history, but are yet creatively shaping others' views on history. This group includes librarians, archivists, curators, historic site workers, reenactors, tour guides, preservationists, and antique store owners, among others.

There are lots of people who don't analyze or investigate history, but who love to read (and virtually memorize) all the available books on a particular subject in history such as World War Two or the Civil War. These people we might call history buffs. Truth be told, however, most history buffs do more than memorize information or jealously guard their historical artifacts. They also actively process it, remember and recall narratives, and tell others about what they have learned. In this sense, they are indeed acting as historians. They are selecting information, analyzing it, even if in the most basic way, and then passing it on to others. Sub-categories of history buffs include anti-quarians, genealogists, History Channel fans, and coin and stamp collectors. History buffs can make great tour guides on family vacations. They like to show up to historical society presentations and challenge historians with questions about lesser-known Civil War regiments. They keep historians hon-est. Nevertheless, history buffs have trouble making it very far in academia, mostly because their focus is too narrow, or they love facts and minutiae more than historiography and interpretation. History buffs like answers more than questions—and for this reason, they tend to like certainty more than creativ-ity, although many do like the creativity of historical fiction. History buffs don't produce much written history, but they consume a lot of it, and make great audiences for other historians.

If we want people to have more applicable, transferrable skills, we should train students to be more like historians and less like history buffs. We should therefore highlight the interpretive side of history, and the many arguments about it. To reconceptualize history as a creative exercise with the goal of teaching everyone how to analyze and interpret sources, we need to recognize that history is not set in place, but can always be re-written. The term "revisionist history" is often used to describe a willful distortion of history. Intentional misrepresentation of the past should of course be avoided, but all good his-tory is revisionist history in the sense that historians are constantly revising their understanding of the past. A scholar of history who only repeats what previous authorities have written, but who comes up with no new insight, is in the true sense not acting as a historian. Such a person is little more than a scribe or a plagiarizer.

The time is ripe for promoting creative historical thinking across the board, for all people, and for all levels of history education. One important reason for this is that the ability to recall facts has lost its power. In past ages, facts were at a premium. In a small village or a remote countryside, knowledge was difficult to find and was precious to hold. Once upon a time, if you did not know an answer to a big historical question, you had to seek out a rare book or a wise man on a mountaintop. Only in recent centuries have people been able to consult a written encyclopedia to find answers to historical questions. Even into the beginning of the twentieth century, educated persons were those who knew a certain set of facts which would distinguish them from the uneducated. But now, of course, in our digital age, facts are super-abundant. We don't need to look far to find facts, and we hardly need to consult wise or educated per-sons to get our fill of facts. If anything, we are overwhelmed with facts and need to learn how to deal with the burden.

Facts and Alternative Facts

The demand for critical, open reflection of the nature of facts and interpretations is also very much a necessary part of our democratic political process. As this book was in progress, Kellyanne Conway, counselor to President Donald Trump, introduced the now famous term "alternative facts." For many, this term signaled a new postmodernism of the right, in which the Trump administration co-opted the denial of truth to serve ideological ends. But why does the term "alternative facts" arouse so much interest, anger, and disbelief?

When it comes to philosophical questions about facts, most historians take a "common sense" approach, which is a kind way of saying they just do not think about the problem very deeply and hope that it will go away. But for all historians, the idea that there are good facts, or true facts, and bad facts, or false facts, is quite common and uncontroversial. Yet the term "alternative facts" must strike even the historian as something a bit odd. "Alternative facts" is a great juxtaposition of concepts. The word "alternative" suggests choice. The word "facts" suggests something solid and true. Together the two words form a perfect tension, almost an oxymoron.

A lot of the incredulous reaction to the term "alternative facts" probably stems from the elision of facts and truth in our language, because in modern English we confuse "facts" and "truth" by treating the words as nearly synonymous. We like to believe that truth claims are singular and exclusive, so there cannot be truth and alternative truth, as if you get to choose between the two. But by one definition, a fact is just a piece of information, and information can be true or false. For example, I can say that I batted .450 in the major leagues last year. That is a piece of information, and in that sense, it is a fact, but it is also not true. We can also imagine situations in which we believe a fact to be true, but on further investigation, it turns out not to be. For instance, a claim like "consuming too much soda causes cancer" is a fact that we might consider true at one point in time, but later discover to be false, or vice-versa.

The term "alternative facts" is upsetting to so many people because it refuses to admit falsification. Even if we disagree about larger interpretations of the world, we like to think that we can at least recognize the same evidence on the ground. In our dominant, empirical, and scientific worldview, we imagine that when we interpret the world around us, we start with observable facts, and then work our way up to theory or interpretation. We still think like a Dickensian schoolmaster if we recite the mantra "Facts! All we need are facts!"

But historians have long recognized that this is not a correct picture of how people think. Facts are shaped by context. Narrative structures and our idiosyncratic predispositions also affect the kinds of facts we look for and what we select to build our interpretations. So, it is not the case that we all encounter the same facts and then only have to argue about interpretations. Instead, we cannot avoid seeing and choosing our own relevant facts within our pre-existing mental frameworks. Interpreting any set of facts requires us to have outside knowledge, ways of organizing and arranging the facts. As historians are fond of saying, "the facts do not interpret themselves."

So, is it the case that one person's facts are another person's "alternative facts"? Are "alternative facts" and regular old facts just another way of saying "my facts and yours"? No, I think "alternative facts" introduce something new to the conversation by suggesting that while my facts and your facts may be in conflict, any set of facts is as good as any other. "Alternative facts," as expressed by Kellyanne Conway, suggests an unwillingness to weigh evidence and work towards a correct interpretation. Employing "alternative facts" is a brusque way of saying that we disagree and are not willing to consider other positions, even if they might be correct. It is the hubris of the conceit of knowledge. The arrival of "alternative facts" and "fake news" highlights the problem of interpretation, and offers us a moment of self-reflection. The public reaction to this whole episode shows that belief in the existence of truth is very much alive in our society. Indeed, if you do not believe in truth, you cannot get all that upset about a term like "alternative facts."

History education, conceived as a creative enterprise, encourages the skills necessary to interpret facts and to recognize that disagreements may lie not in observation, but in theory or applied metaphors of interpretation.

Most of the commentary on Trump's historical understanding has focused on his errors of simple historical facts. But this misses the point. Trump's populist view of history is not an argument based on evidence, but a set of feelings projected backwards onto a selection of convenient facts. Populists are less concerned about how things were than they are concerned with how things should have been. So, for example, when right-wing populists study the American Civil War, they don't seek explanation of the past; they seek justification for their present beliefs.

Experience Provides Metaphors for Creative Interpretation

Finding historical facts is an easy business, but explaining them is difficult creative work. In the deluge of historical information, we need a filtering device, something that does more than simply place evidence in order. In my mind, all the best historians or history teachers have had a wide variety of life experiences which give them the ability to imagine another time and place and interpret it in a creative way. Instead of restating facts in front of a classroom, they explain the facts as part of a recognizable pattern. They relate one thing in terms of another, and thereby present history through metaphors that link us in common understanding.

As a graduate student at Florida State University, I found the Civil War lectures of Dr. Jim Jones so clear and so convincing that I could easily imagine myself in the midst of battle. Sometimes, while listening to him lecture, I came to believe the year truly was 1863. Professor Jones knew all of the facts about the Civil War that he could reasonably know. What made him a particularly good storyteller, however, was that he could use his own experience to find lasting metaphors and analogies that the audience could relate to. For example, he used a football analogy to describe the "wing-formation" of Union soldiers advancing on the Confederate position in Corinth, Mississippi. He drew on his travel experiences to bring himself into the story by way of comparison. For example, he likened the twentieth-century Mongolian railroad to the Confederate railroad. From experience, he knew that the tracks of the Mongolian railroad were of a different gauge than the Chinese railroad track. The design was intentional, so that trains could not pass easily across the border, but had to instead stop and unload their cargo of people and goods to be transferred to the other set of rails. This travel annoyance was actually part of defensive measures to prevent the Chinese from invading. If it slowed down tourists, it would slow down armies, as well. Railroads in the American South also had a variety of different gauges. This, however, was an accidental feature, the result of the patchwork growth of the Southern railroad network in the 1850s. The result was not that the Union soldiers were kept out of the South, but that Confederates experienced all kinds of internal railroad delays as people and goods had to switch trains.

In reconstructing the past, travelers have more experiences to draw on and more comparisons to make between what they know and what might have happened. It is no coincidence that great travelers become great storytellers (the great Greek historian Herodotus, sometimes called "the father of history," collected stories while traveling), nor is it coincidence that there is a metaphorical link between traveling abroad and investigating the past, as in the saying "the past is like a foreign country." Historians can be likened, metaphorically, to cosmopolitan travelers in strange lands. The French historian Fernand Braudel explained that historians and travelers study something outside themselves with the result that they come to understand something inside. Braudel wrote:

> Live in London for a year and you will not know much about England. But by contrast, in light of what has surprised you, you will suddenly have come to understand some of the most deep-seated and characteristic aspects of France [or your own country of origin], things you did not know before because you knew them too well. With regard to the present, the past too is a way of distancing yourself.[7]

Another one of my great teachers, Dr. William Cohen, also seemed to always find a story from his own life to illustrate a historical point. Whatever Dr. Cohen taught, it seemed that the lectures were autobiographical. He could relate to the nineteenth century by having us consider a moment in his life in the twentieth. I began to joke with fellow classmates that his courses should no longer be listed in the college catalog as "The Civil War" or "The History of American Slavery," but rather should carry titles like "An Autobiography of William Cohen With Brief References to the Civil War." In one memorable example from a lecture, Dr. Cohen explained that in the 1950s, when he was going through basic training in the U.S. Army, soldiers were still made to fasten bayonets and charge a dummy bag during drill. Why, he asked us, would bayonet charges be useful in the age of machine guns and nuclear weapons? The answer is that bayonets would probably not be useful, but drill was about more than military tactics; it was intended to instill in the soldiers a strong obedience to their superior's orders. As I pondered the Civil War and the First World War, drill took on a new meaning in my mind. Drill was not only for exercise and improving skill with weapons and tactics; it was a psychological tool. I recognized that there could be layers of meaning in history, hidden cultural practices, structures of organization or control. And while my professor could have simply stated that conclusion for me without incorporating an anecdote from the 1950s, his personal story provided an unforgettable mental image. I began to look for underlying causes of things, hidden themes of history.

Metaphors Give Flavor to Historical Writing

It is certainly correct that when we encounter data that appears to contradict our metaphors and narrative constructions, we are again and again reminded to check the theory of our interpretation. In the conventional view, historians seek data, and then interpret it as objectively as possible. But it is impossible to act on data without normative claims or concerns, which drive our search. Discovered facts must be mapped on to our pre-existing knowledge and ways of seeing the world. People choose metaphors, derived from their experiences, to explain the data. Then, they extend the metaphors to see how useful and consistent they might be. Logical coherence determines the quality of the metaphor. Metaphors are essential in reconstructing the past because they provide a logic to understand cause and effect.

Good historical writing goes beyond just the facts, and includes plausible metaphors to shape interpretations. Notice the metaphors at work in the following example from David Christian, who presents a beautiful analogy between astronomy and history:

> In the early universe, gravity took hold of clouds of atoms, and sculpted them into stars and galaxies . . . by a sort of social gravity, cities and states were sculpted from scattered communities of farmers. As farming populations gathered in larger and denser communities, interactions between different groups increased and the social pressure rose until, in a striking parallel with star formation, new structures suddenly appeared, together with a new level of complexity. Like stars, cities and states reorganize and energize the smaller objects within their gravitational field.[8]

Cities, we know, developed through a combination of human decision-making and geographical chance, while star formation is pure physics. By framing the development of cities in terms of the interplay of physical forces, Christian asks us to imagine the complex processes as a sort of determined outcome of science. To what extent this analogy is correct, I cannot say, since I am neither an expert on star formation nor an expert on the formation of early cities. In a sense, Christian does not actually explain star formation, nor does he explain the formation of cities. But by likening them to each other, he imparts meaning. Each process becomes clearer as we recognize their isomorphic quality.

In another example, the historian Joseph A. Amato writes that "Local historians must collect and preserve the primary and secondary documents of their locale. Over time, this can turn into a pressing obligation and even a matter of despair, as time sweeps things clean."[9] In Amato's metaphor, time is like a broom, and the memory of the past is like a litter of facts or a thousand flecks of dust. In this metaphor, old things do not vanish on their own accord, but it is time itself which plays an active role in the death of the past. For things forgotten, people speak of the dustbin or trash heap of history. For history remembered, they speak of the weight of stories, the burden of the past.

These metaphors are not just passing, randomly chosen devices for creative writing. There are in fact certain kinds of historical interpretations that are so laden with metaphors that it would be nearly impossible to speak about the subject without using some kind of metaphor. Immigration historians, for example are fond of water metaphors. They write about streams and flows of immigrants, and waves of immigration.[10] They say that the first immigrants formed an anchor, and that a chain migration followed. They also use botanical metaphors to talk about how immigrants were "uprooted" or "transplanted." These metaphors shape new research as historians continue to look for the same kinds of things.

Economic history, meanwhile, is essentially one giant attempt to convince others of the proper metaphors to explain the abstraction of the market process. The economy has been described as a revolving wheel that needs to keep spinning, or a garden that needs tilling. Some see it as a giant machine with many gears, while others call it an ecosystem that is naturally self-adjusting. Some see economics as a competition between states, or a zero-sum game. Economists also speak of peaks and valleys, troughs, and cycles. There are "bubbles, bears, bulls, bliss points, sunspots, cobwebs, and dirty floats."[11] A popular Keynesian idea is "pump-priming," even though opponents of Keynesianism might just as easily describe the policy as "crowding out" the wealth of potential investments. Economic historians look for data that matches the logic of known metaphors.

Metaphorical language is even at play in how historians think about the methods of their own discipline. For example, two of the most common metaphors for explaining how historians understand human agency as a driving force in history are "History from the Bottom Up" and "Great Man History." In the first conception, history is conceived of as a process influenced by the actions of millions upon millions of people. The cumulative actions of the masses, those at the bottom of society, are responsible for the larger processes of historical change. "Great Man History" argues the opposite, that what the majority of people do from day to day has little actual effect on the grand course of history, but that the important decisions of politicians, inventors, and other people with leading roles in society effect the true "turning points" of history.

Without metaphor in history, we wouldn't have interpretations. Without metaphor, history would just be a set of facts, but in that case, it wouldn't really be history after all. The facts we choose and the way we interpret them reflect our own experiences and what we already know about the world. An openness to the frameworks of interpretation and the experiences of others, allows us to entertain alternative explanations. When conversation is possible, we can sort through facts and alternative facts together and locate more convincing interpretations of the past. It is in this sense that history is and must be a social discipline.

Conclusion

I've argued in this chapter that interpretations, theory, and metaphor are what matter for historians, and that learning facts is not the true goal of history education.

History departments across the country advertise the usefulness of the discipline, usually through appeals to its practicality. It is true that history education improves our reading comprehension and our writing, but seldom is historical content directly useful or applicable. Instead, it is the lessons of working through problems, of analysis, that help us to consider other metaphors and theories of interpretation that makes us better able to encounter the world. In other words: it is the general, not specific, lessons of history that are important. It is not the facts, but the process, that needs to be taught more.

There is a largely forgotten gem of an article by J.W. Swain, published over the course of various issues of a philosophy journal in 1923, that describes historical thinking as the engine for developing new philosophies and new ways of looking at the world. It is this view that I find more appealing and more accurate than the idea that knowing historical content, i.e. facts, make us better people or better scholars. Swain writes:

> History has but little to teach in a direct way that has an immediately practical value: the man of affairs will not profit much directly from the so-called "lessons of history," though he may get suggestions from other men who have faced his problems: but a study of the historians will bring the reader's mind into contact with other philosophies and points of view, and thus broaden and deepen his view of the world. If he finds one whose point of view agrees with his own, the facts presented by this historian will give strength to this view, and fortify him in his endeavors to make this view prevail. In case it is a profound and fruitful philosophy, much of value will surely result. This is what is meant by the statement that while he deals with the past the historian is creating the future.[12]

Notes

1. Richard A. Knaak, *The Legend of Huma* (Lake Geneva, WI: TSR, 1988); Frank Herbert, *Dune* (Philadelphia, PA: Chilton Books, 1965); Jon Fasman, *The Geographer's Library* (London: Penguin Books, 2006), 21. The historian in Fasman's novel spends a lifetime writing a local history text, which, as Fasman explains, becomes increasingly focused on minutiae: "The more he talked about [his] project, the longer it became: a history of a town comprising every event in the town's existence fully researched and retold in precisely the same amount of time the initial event lasted." The extreme version of this can be seen in science fantasy novels like Knaak's *The Legend of Huma*, where the ageless and exacting historian Astinus works from dawn to dusk, year in, year out, isolated in his ivory tower, recording the chronicles of his world. Similarly, the psychohistorians in the fantasy world *Dune* use computers to chart all possible human actions, thereby deriving a perfect understanding of past and future developments.

2. Allen Nevins, *The Gateway to History* (Garden City, NY: Anchor Books, 1962 [original edition 1938]), 67.

3. E.H. Carr, *What Is History?* (New York: Vintage Press, 1961), 14.

4. Thomas Andrews and Flannery Burke, "What Does It Mean to Think Historically" *Perspectives on History* (January 2007) https://www.historians.org/publications-and-directories/perspectives-on-history/january-2007/what-does-it-mean-to-think-historically, accessed March 21, 2018; Bruce A. VanSledrigt, "What Does It Mean to Think Historically . . . and How Do You Teach It?" *Social Education* 68: 3, 230–233. The journal *Historically Speaking*, which ran from 1999–2013, carried many articles on historical thinking. Stephane Levesque, *Thinking Historically: Educating Students for the Twenty-First Century* (Toronto: University of Toronto Press, 2008); Peter N. Stearns, Peter Seixas, and Sam Wineburg, eds., *Knowing, Teaching and Learning History: National and International Perspectives* (New York: NYU Press, 2000); S.G. Grant, *History Lessons: Teaching, Learning, and Testing in U.S. High School Classrooms* (Mahwah, NJ: Lawrence Erlbaum, 2003).

5. Sam Wineburg, *Historical Thinking and Other Unnatural Acts: Charting the Future of Teaching the Past* (Philadelphia, PA: Temple University Press, 2001).

6. R.[obin] G. Collingwood, *The Philosophy of History*, Historical Association Leaflet no. 79, London: Bell, 1930, page 3. Cited in Marnie Hughes-Warrington, *Fifty Key Thinkers on History* (Routledge, 2015), 39–40.

7. Fernand Braudel, *On History* (Chicago: University of Chicago Press, 1982 [original in French, 1969]), 37.

8. David Christian, *Maps of Time: An Introduction to Big History* (Berkeley, CA: University of California Press, 2004), 245.

9. Joseph A. Amato, *Rethinking Home: A Case for Writing Local History* (Berkeley, CA: University of California Press, 2002), 9.

10. Jon Gjerde, "New Growth on Old Vines: The State of the Field: The Social History of Immigration to and Ethnicity in the United States" *Journal of American Ethnic History* 18:4 (July 1999), 40–46.

11. Arjo Klamer and Thomas C. Leonard, "So What's an Economic Metaphor," in Philip Mirowski, editor. *Natural Images in Economic Thought* (Cambridge: Cambridge University Press, 1994), 23. Also useful on this topic are: Mary S. Morgan, *The World in the Model* (Cambridge: Cambridge University Press, 2012), and Deirde McCloskey, "Metaphors Economists Live By" *Social Research* 62:2 (Summer 1995), 215–237. www.deirdremccloskey.com/docs/pdf/Article_146.pdf, accessed March 21, 2018.

12. Joseph Ward Swain, "What Is History? V" *The Journal of Philosophy*, 20:13 (June 21, 1923), 340, 337–349, specifically 349.

Section II

Practical Strategies for Students to Become Creative Historians

Section II is intended primarily for students who wish to become historians, but might also be useful for those who already consider themselves historians and who would like to improve their ability to think creatively. This section consists of four chapters. Chapter 4 is about what historians should read. My short answer is that they should read everything they want to—and more, but they should not feel pressured by reading lists that others prescribe for them. Chapter 5 gives advice about how to write and how to think about writing. The key to writing creative history, I argue, is to write often and to maintain multiple research projects. Chapter 6 presents networking and entrepreneurship as the neglected skills of successful creative historians. Chapter 7, a story of my experiences learning the history of my property, intends to inspire others to see history all around them.

The advice given in this section may not apply to everyone, but hopefully it will serve as fruitful ground for new historians thinking about their own research strategies. For readers in graduate school, I have one essential piece of advice: you need to think of yourself as a historian who is getting a degree, and not as a continuing student. Many people have difficulty with this transition from student to independent scholar. The difference between the two is that a student looks to others for motivation and a plan. An independent historian already knows in what direction they want to go.

4   How Creative Historians Read and Research

One of my graduate school professors once told me that all serious scholars read *The Economist*. Logically, I knew this could not be the case. *The Economist* is a fine source for information, as is NPR, the *New York Times*, and the *Journal of American History*, but these shouldn't be your only sources, and they are not essential reading material. Many perfectly competent, even great, serious scholars never get information from any of these sources, and yet they do just fine. If someone designates a source as essential, they unwittingly close themselves off from other sources and interpretations. Thus, it is important to assert with confidence that there are no essential books—there are only good books and bad books. Besides, if you were to read everything contributors to the *American Historical Review* label "required reading," you might never actually get to your research. The goal of every creative historian is to produce new material. Since time is finite, productive historians don't try to read the entire canon of all the great books. To read like a creative historian, the first thing is to realize that you can't read everything.

In my experience, creative historians are omnivorous readers, interested in all kinds of books and articles. Creativity comes from curiosity, and I find that I learn more in a good evening spent browsing the library at random than I would sitting down to read one great book. Books chosen at random can be useful as examples of writing—not only for subject matter, but also for style. To encourage creativity, spend time reading without purpose—be like a wanderer in the woods—and you will come across new species of literaria. You will discover that reading without purpose actually does have a purpose: to survey a variety of fields, introducing yourself to new kinds of literature. It's not just a matter of encountering facts and topics of other genres, but also a matter of seeing entirely different ways of thinking that writers of other fields and genres are likely to possess. So, read for knowledge and not for word count. Read for pleasure, and not out of a sense of duty. Don't feel obligated to finish every book you pick up: give up on some of them and cast them aside. The right books are not the ones you are forced to buy for school, or the ones your advisor assigns you. The right books cannot be prescribed to you but must be chosen by you, slowly, over a lifetime, as you discover those that shape you and speak to you.

Interesting sources that inspire creativity are often within reach, but hidden behind a shelf, or in a closed-off room; they are there—it just requires an extra step to find them. I assume that if all the interesting books were easy to find, we would be less excited by discovering them. My own search for interesting books began in elementary school. As a child, I was convinced that the school librarian could answer many of my questions about the world. After all, the librarian was an adult, and I trusted adults. But I lost this trust already in second grade, when the librarian allowed me only to check out books from the fiction section of the library. The non-fiction section, she told me, was reserved for students in third grade and higher. Of course, all of the books I really wanted to read were on the non-fiction shelves. I think, then, that my love of history developed out of a desire to satisfy my curiosity for what I could not have access to. In fourth grade, I checked out all of the Isaac Asimov books on the planets. I broke free from prescribed classroom readings and read what I found more interesting. I usually skimmed what was assigned for class, and then set about learning other subjects on my own. Ironically, my desire to learn new things made me a bad student, since I was not focused on work for class. I kept up this pattern all the way through graduate school, and in the long run I had read so much more than what had been assigned in class.

What I discovered is that if you make reading enjoyable, and you read to satisfy your own curiosity, you will always benefit from it and learn to incorporate new knowledge in new, interesting ways. Make a game out of reading. Consider it a quest or a kind of strength training program. Do whatever you have to do to make sure that you spend time at it. I like to read a book in the place in which it was written, or at least in the country or region where the story takes place. After Hugo at the steps of the Cathedral de Notre Dame and Marx in the square in Brussels, I'll never forget them. I associate books with places. Sometimes I discovered a writer out of place. I discovered the historian J.H. Plumb, for example, in a book sale on the Alexanderstrasse in Berlin. When you discover Ferdinand Tonnies in Niedersachsen or Galileo inside a medieval castle on the Mediterranean coast, you can feel the air, and the book seems to make more sense, have more impact. The stories and arguments grow from their native soil.

To be a creative historian, however, you do sometimes need to read with a focus. When a topic strikes your interest and you think you might be able to say something new about it, you should try to read everything you can about that topic. By reading voraciously, mercilessly, I believe it is possible to become an expert on a topic fairly quickly. Being an expert consists of knowing a lot of content, but it is also an attitude that you take towards your subject. Remember that everyone who ever became an expert on something started in the same state of ignorance. The physicist Richard Feynman, for example, often told people that he was an expert lock picker. As a consequence, people brought him locks and challenged him to pick them. He learned to pick locks to meet the challenges. Similarly, I know someone who informed all of his friends that he spoke Spanish, when he only really knew a few words of the language. But, over the course of a few years, as word spread that this friend spoke Spanish, he was forced to practice it. In both instances, simply declaring that they were experts was sufficient for eventually gaining competence and later, perhaps, expertise.

A unique reading list will help you develop a unique set of competencies to inspire creative thought. Cultivate a deep, wide understanding across a variety of topics. Incorporate and synthesize new knowledge, or cast it off. The worst thing you can do (to hamper your creativity, that is) is listen to the news and involuntarily gravitate towards the mean of society. Creative scholars are seldom informed citizens. They don't have time to be both. The news repeats a standard set of voices, limiting the range of possible opinions and insufficiently representing the divergence from a prescribed center. Instead, you should break free from the average and read everything that strikes you as curious. Perhaps that means you develop an interest in Norwegian literature, 1970s sci-fi, and local histories. Anything you read now may be used later, since a good historian is also picking up facts and frameworks along the trail. Time spent with bad books is not necessarily wasted. Bad books are useful as guides for how not to write or argue. Amateur histories, meanwhile, while of mixed quality, are useful as examples of how people outside of academia think about the past.

Ask fellow historians to name their favorite or most influential read. Seldom will they tell you about a book that is only a waste of time. A "most influential book" also often serves to give an organizing principle to a scholar's thought, so you might learn to read their work as a reflection of the ideas they learned elsewhere. For example, I like the travel writing of Simon Winchester and the folklore analyses of Henry Glassie. Both influence my writing and thought in implicit and explicit ways. The first speaks to a desire to move about and meet new people, the second highlights the need for community and the essential social practices that carry on traditions. I like narrative history like Alfred Young's *The Shoemaker and the Revolution*; the theoretical overviews of history, like Peter Burke's *History & Social Theory*; and radical works like Ivan Illich's *Deschooling Society* and Paul Feyerabend's *Against Method*. I like classic works of history by Francis Parkman, Henri Pirenne, and Carlo Ginzburg. And, no surprise, I like the quirky, creative types of books like Lawrence Wechsler's *Mr. Wilson's Cabient of Wonder*, David Weitzman's *May Backyard History Book*, and anything by Eric Sloane.

Digital Sources

Books, of course, are just one kind of source that creative historians should engage. Much of what historians read today is online in the form of history websites, blogs, and digitally accessible journals. Digital archives compliment and in some cases even replace physical archives. Search databases like Google books, Hathitrust, and HeinOnline, among many others, provide historians with an unprecedented power to locate relevant sources. These databases are still relatively new, and in truth, historians are just beginning to use them. This is really the first generation to be able to use these sources to draw narrative lines, to con-nect greater swaths of evidence to check earlier interpretations of events. This allows historians to digest a greater array of sources in a shorter amount of time.

Like any new historical method, digital historical research has much to prom-ise but cannot solve all practical problems. Historians will still need to debate the evidence and do the work of piecing it together in new ways. Blinded by a superabundance of data, we might lose our humility about our ability to know. We still need to read deeply, and patiently consider what meaning we give to evidence. Creative historical thinking still requires the ability to concentrate for extended periods of time. To focus, we sometimes need less technology, not more. We need to learn to sit still again, to become comfortable with the dis-comfort of our own thoughts, to spend hours away from screens and soundbites. The most neglected lesson is the lesson in becoming free of the technology that overwhelms our ability to think by ourselves and for ourselves. Don't mistake my caution about digital history as a rejection of new technology, however. I might want to live in a log cabin, but it had better have an Internet connection.

Digital tools are now indispensable for historical research. At their best, digital tools free up historians to do less tedious work and more critical think-ing. Better tools and increased competition in academia also means that historians are producing more written material per person now than at any other time in the past. Although there is much bad history written today, I would argue that the history written today is also, on average, better informed than at any other point in time. A big reason for this is digital technology. Tools for data analysis and tools for producing graphs, charts, and maps make research and production stages easier. Online materials are publicly available for all researchers to use, so it is less likely as a historian that you will find a completely unique piece of knowledge online. But search engines and crowd-sourced questions can help you locate information more quickly. Digital tools help to narrow down the source of new knowledge. They may lead you to papers in archives, and while these are generally organized and labeled, not all information they contain is readily apparent through a catalog search. Dis-covering new information requires that you dig deeper than historians have in the past. It requires that you sort through lesser-known collections in lesser-known archives. To gain access to new information, you may need to be more persistent than others, or more courageous. You will need to gain the trust of archivists and bother them to take a look at their unprocessed or hidden col-lections. New discoveries take patience.

Research as Pressure Over Time

Creative historians must have persistence, as well as curiosity. Many of my his-torical finds in archives have come from taking risks and being stubbornly per-sistent. I once flew to Copenhagen to find a collection of papers that only had the briefest mention in an online search. I arrived with no contacts in Den-mark and with no idea that the country was just starting a three-day holiday. I had planned to spend five days in the archives, but the holiday cut that down to two days. A helpful English-speaking archivist listened to me as I described what I was looking for. On the first day in the archives, I had no luck. On the second day, I kept up my search and found the papers I was looking for. These papers were not where I expected to find them, but were in a mislabeled folder, in a different box than the catalog suggested. I discovered papers from the Lincoln administration in Denmark, in a place no other American historian was likely to look.[1]

Creative research also requires persistent work on a topic over time. To become an expert, you need to focus on a narrow topic for an extended period of time. Sometimes it is planning and precision that work best, but don't discount brute force. In the 1960s, my mentor visited all of the county courthouses in the two northern rows of counties in Iowa, gathered land records, coded them, and used early computers to derive statistics that would prove that Native Americans in the area had been less than fully compensated for the value of their land.[2]

Research sometimes requires time and effort on the geologic scale. About four or five times a year, a collection agency gives me a call and asks for "Michael" but they really want to talk to Michael C____, some deadbeat who used to have my phone number. Like a good historian in an extremely slowly unfolding research project, I am charting the life course of Mr. C. Instead of getting mad about the "wrong number," I now look forward to the calls and any new information I might accidently learn without, of course, unethically and or illegally posing as this other person. This is probably the slowest-developing research project I can imagine.

Persistent research leads to new ways of seeing the world. It re-shapes our brain's networks. A common symptom of "dissertation fever" is that the afflicted person can relate his or her topic to anything whatsoever. I know the feeling, and I've seen it in others. I once wrote a small book about Dutch brick houses in Michigan. For four months, I drove across the west Michigan countryside looking for brick houses. When I moved to Florida a year later, I still imagined that I saw the same kinds of houses on the landscape. A friend of mine can relate anything to late nineteenth-century Unitarianism, and another sees the price of gold as the main cause of all fluctuations in the economy. In a college class, I once assigned an article by Scott Nelson Reynolds, a historian who argues that the recession of 2008 had a strong parallel in the panic of 1873. The class debated the article and discussed the merits of the argument. It was a strong article, they agreed. But I noted that Reynolds had been studying the recession of 1873 for years, so he was bound to see parallels. In fact, I imagine Reynolds could probably relate the panic of the 1870s to my niece's birthday party. Creative research requires, however, that you can eventually leave a topic behind and focus on new topics with other forms of analysis. Once you have mastered a topic, it is easy to dwell on it forever, repeating your research and never moving on. In other words, it is easy to get comfortable with the knowledge you have.

Reading and Research Not a Lonely Pursuit

Reading and research should not be a lonely process. The goal is eventually to bring your newfound knowledge back into conversation with others. Talk about your favorite books and test your research ideas by telling others about them. Tell your fellow graduate students, tell your neighbor, tell the barista at Starbucks, tell whoever you can. If they ignore you, then maybe your idea is not worth pursuing. If their ears prick up, and they ask for more, maybe you have found an interesting topic. You must enjoy the topic, but it must also be appealing to others. When it is both, then you can feed off the energy of telling others what you have discovered. Months after you think you have finished writing, that barista is going to ask you about your project, and maybe you will have something new to tell them.

In the end, I believe that it is reading and research that makes a good, creative historian. Sometimes history graduate students tell me that they want to become professors who only teach. They say they do not want to be pressured to publish. But I struggle to relate to this. To me, publishing is exciting, not loathsome, and the idea of a lecturer who does no research strikes me as a bit odd because so much of what I know about history I have learned through firsthand research. Research and the creation of historical interpretations is essential to understanding history as a discipline. Through your own research, you learn the difficulty of ascertaining facts; you build tentative conclusions at first and work toward near certainty, always maintaining a willingness to reconsider your views. Knowledge gained firsthand through research is something you can use to argue about history. I can tell you what various textbook authors *think* about a subject, but it is a difficult thing for me to *argue* from the position of one of those authors unless I've done the work myself to reach similar conclusions. Research gives us uniqueness in our views. I don't want to listen to somebody lecture about what other people think about history; I want to listen to somebody lecture about what *they* think about history—what they *know*, through research, experience, and time spent mulling it over.

Widely read people, with experiences as researchers, tend to find creative solutions for problems. They are people you want on your team. If we can get the creative thinking concept to catch on and spread across the country, from college down to kindergarten, then the next generation of history professors will all embrace and enjoy research instead of fearing and avoiding it. Cultivating creativity from a young age will lead to a more widespread appreciation for and participation in hands-on/firsthand research. Maybe "publish or perish" will become "Research and rejoice," or at the very least, "publish and prosper" (something positive instead of something threatening).

Notes

1. Michael J. Douma and Anders Bo Rasmussen, "The Danish St. Croix Project: Revisiting the Lincoln Colonization Program with Foreign-Language Sources" *American Nineteenth Century History* 15:3 (2014): 311–342.
2. Robert P. Swierenga, *Acres for Cents: Delinquent Tax Auctions in Frontier Iowa* (Santa Barbara, CA: Praeger, 1976).

5 How Creative Historians Write

Imagine two men who have entered an upcoming bicycle race. The first man buys the latest specialized racing bicycle and a lot of expensive, tight-fitting clothes. He also reads cycling magazines and owns all the latest gear. Every once in a while, on a nice day, he goes for a ride around town. By contrast, a second man inherited his father's old ten-speed Schwinn, and he pedals it a dozen miles to work nearly every day. Who here is the real cyclist? Who is likely to fare better in the upcoming race? By studying but not researching or writing history, aspiring historians make an analogous mistake. Historians need to write often—every day if they can. Strength comes from repetitive pressure and exercise.

Creative research and creative writing are two sides of the same coin. Many people confuse creative writing with "Creative Writing," a class offered in high school and college English departments. Many of my former students had taken such courses and as a result they wrote the most flowery, over-wrought, descriptive nonsense I've ever read. They put words before ideas. I discovered that their word choice was indeed creative, but the content of their ideas was not. Real creative writing puts ideas first and recognizes that the words are a tool of communication, not an end in themselves.[1]

In thinking about the past, you are really organizing your present conscious-ness. So historians who do not write, who perhaps *cannot* write, might be charged with having nothing on their minds. Writer's block tends not to be a problem, however, for those who do research and have something to say. One way to cure writer's block is to change your focus. Either zoom in or zoom out. If you are studying a brick, and you have said everything you think you can say about the brick—that it is reddish-colored, rectangular, and weighs about seven pounds—you might say more by looking closely at its chemistry, or you can step back and see that the brick is part of a wall. Maybe the bricks are arranged in a pattern on the wall. The wall is part of a building, and the build-ing is part of streetscape, a cultural competence, and an architectural style.

Creative historical writing involves working through problems, and this requires time and effort. You will not always have the answers when you begin to write. And, if you wait for the answers before you write, you might never get started. Too often, history students are taught to propose a question, then go out and seek answers in the sources. A recent book states "the design of a good historical research project begins with the formulation of a question."[2] Well, not in my experience. Sometimes we are deep into our research before we find the question that we are ultimately going to pose, or indeed the point that we wish to make. It is simply false that all research begins with a question. I don't research old chairmaking because I have a specific or even a general question about the history of chairs, but because I am only interested in knowing more about them. Sometimes, perhaps most of the time, we don't know even what the proper questions to ask are until we look at the sources. The folklorist Henry Glassie explained it this way:

> Study without hypotheses, and you might reach no conclusion. Or you might come to any conclusion with no means for its evaluation. But these are caveats inappropriately imported from natural to social sciences. Culture is not a problem with a solution. There are no conclusions. Studying people involves refining understanding, not achieving final proof. Perhaps if you observe people as though they were planets or orchids, proceeding without hypotheses is foolhardy, but that was not my intention.[3]

In agreement with Glassie, I believe that historical research does not always begin with questions or hypotheses, but arrives at them. Furthermore, I think that historians generally do not walk around with fully formed definitions of things like "culture" or "society." Grant applications sometimes ask a scholar to explain in precise terms what they plan on writing about. This seems to present a bit of paradox for those who keep an open mind about where the sources might lead them. As a colleague once told me: "If I knew what I was going to say, it wouldn't be a research project."

Philosophically, definitions of broad concepts are quite difficult to nail down, and if we had to define all of our terms perfectly, we would never get anywhere. I've heard it said that if a word has a history, it cannot have a precise definition. Words like "democracy," "freedom," and "capitalism" are examples of this type. To understand these words, we can't rely on a simple, single dictionary definition, as there are bound to be many competing, even conflicting, definitions. Instead, we need to historicize these words; that is, we need to understand the history of where these words came from and how they have been used over time. It is history which gives words complex, overlapping, even contradictory meaning. Words that describe historical periods and movement are often of this kind. This is why philosopher of history Frank Ankersmit can write that: "To require fixed meanings for words like the Cold War or Mannerism would amount to requiring that historical debate should stop. Historical writing does not presuppose, but results in definitions."[4] Knowing the meanings of these terms, and knowing what questions to ask about them, is often the result of research. At any rate, I don't wish to belabor this point, but only wish to state that it is better that historians write first, and then work to improve their writing, than it is for them to wait until they have all of the answers before they begin to write. Philosophers wrestle with definitions, and scientists fret about controls for their experiments, but a historian must dive right in to the sources and dig around.

Writing Is the Shaping of Ideas

I think of writing history as painting reality. There is a framework and a canvas that determine the limits of the project. The painting is impressionistic, not a perfect representation. The number of facts a historian has in his or her palette is limited to the number of facts he or she can possess.[5] Slowly, a historian's pencil to the paper forms a book like a brush to the canvas forms a painting. Or, to use another metaphor, a historian shapes a book like a sculptor shapes a block of stone. This work is never without flaws. In some ways, those of us who make the most mistakes are ultimately the ones who show the most creativity and make the most progress. Writing is like rolling dough. You begin with a lump of ideas, and with each pass of the dough roller, the dough is pressed into shape. The dough never settles exactly as planned, and you are bound to make a mess along the way.

Few people find writing easy. It is a battle of your mind against itself. In writing this book, sentences were ripped apart and paragraphs came together either in a flurry of inspiration or through painstaking piecework. This bit of text began its life here. Another was born in Chapter 3, found itself pressed into Chapter 4, and was then deleted altogether. The remains of cast-off fragments of writing later found their place. Other than Jack Kerouac, no one writes a book straight through from start to finish. Instead, writers press their ideas into shapes—shapes determined by a recognizable system of sentences, paragraphs, and chapters, fit into forms like essays, books, booklets, and treatises.

One must overcome the desire to know everything about a topic before trying to explain it on paper. In writing history, you learn that what you are doing is not setting out an air-tight cases, but are instead arguing for a likely view, given the parameters of your knowledge, based on the sources you have encountered. It is absolutely crucial to recognize that in historical writing, you can state that you don't know something for certain. While a thesis to an historical work should not waver, there is plenty of room within an argument to explain that sources are unclear about small points in the story. There is something of a mystery in historical explanation. If you explain every step of the story, you do all the work for the reader, and you make it almost too easy. Instead of trying to form perfect links between all possible pieces of evidence in a story, you should instead honestly describe the contours of possible knowledge, so that you get as close to an accurate image as possible. Speculation, estimation, and bridging the narrative are all parts of the historian's toolkit, and they are not unethical if done properly and clearly explained. All history requires leaps of faith between pieces of evidence. If those leaps are too great, your story will not be believable, or readers will consider that you could have found a more likely path of connection.

Creative history writing does not require genius. It is more a function of hard work, experience, and curiosity. I have many friends from graduate school who are probably smarter than I am, but they find themselves unable to write anything original. Many of them struggle to transition from student to scholar. Good students appease their teachers and get good grades, but good creative scholars are the avant-garde, looking to challenge reigning interpretations. Afraid to make mistakes, some historians work so slowly that they never produce anything. Their unwritten work sounds incredible, and it might win them grant funding or admission into a good program. But all too often, the ideas that sounded great in unwritten form remain unwritten. When I read a CV that lists grant after grant, years of fellowships and support at top institutions, but no published research, I shake my head and wonder what this person has been up to all these years.[6]

The biggest mistake in historical writing is that so much of it lacks a real thesis. Too much historical writing is merely gap-filler. Gap-fillers are writings that address a narrow topic solely because the topic has not been studied. A satirical history of England justifies its appearance by "consoling" the reader, only using facts that are commonly known. The book jokes that: "*No other history does this.*"[7] Gap-filling in history probably has the equivalent of back-filling in anthropology. Internet journalism in anthropology includes articles arguing that the discovery of one thing or another pushes back human's use of tools to a time period that is earlier than what was previously thought. But that last statement should raise a red flag: thought by whom? Is there a consensus view on this topic? Far too many dissertations are of the form "I argued that X happened." Only slightly better is "My dissertation argues that 'X' happened, and this is how it happened." In many examples, though, no one has ever denied that X had occurred, so the first part of the argument is useless. History writing needs to do more than tell us that something happened; it should explain why it happened and why it is important for us to know that it happened.

Likewise, published articles are suspect when authors justify themselves by stating that they merely covered a neglected topic or that they complicate rather than clarify historical change. Similarly, a revival of articles on a particular topic does not justify the composition of more articles on the same or similar topics. Instead, solid, good history has the ability to overturn established views on important topics; it clarifies but does not complicate.[8] The goal of original history is not to make just any contribution to the literature but to make a *valuable* contribution. Stating that your argument is more complex than others' arguments is nothing more than a strategy for avoiding presenting a true thesis. And if your main idea is so incredibly obvious that no one could oppose it or think otherwise, then you have still failed to offer anything of true value. Finally, the justification should not be so broad as to be meaningless. How many books about narrow topics include the subtitle "and the Making of the Modern World" in an attempt to justify the importance of a minor historical theme? The only thing worse than historians' overuse of the subtitle "and the Making of the Modern World" is puns of the same. I don't know what my next book project will be, but I'm considering "Vampires, Tents, Fences, and the Staking of the Modern World" or "French Bakeries and the Caking of the Modern World." What about "A History of Politicians, Thieves, and the Taking of the Modern World"?

Good writing is a reflection of a sharp mind, while poor writing in history is often a consequence of a naïve theory of how history happens. Naïve thinkers imagine that things were invented once, only very recently, and close to where they live. They think that particular periods in history had clear beginnings and endings and can be distinguished from each other by clear dates. Naïve thinkers believe ethical systems in the past were necessarily worse than ethical systems at present. They can make simple mistakes like thinking the First Reformed Church of Chicago was *the* very first Reformed church in the world.

Some people want to see historical change as indicated by a single event rather than as a gradual process. They want to know precisely when the Baroque period began, or when the Renaissance ended. They overestimate the importance of a single local event and mistake the arrival of the first local automobile or the first local celebration of a holiday as the very first arrival of an automobile anywhere, or the very first celebration of a particular holiday anywhere. Akin to the naïve view of history is the belief that if you personally are unaware of sources to write a history, said sources must not exist. Naïveté in this sense is a form of solipsistic ignorance of the knowledge that others might give.

No better is the writer who calls all opposing views "monolithic" and all of his own views "nuanced," or who argues that everything needs to be understood as "the product of larger social forces," as if such a statement in itself says anything. It is a similar sort of straw man that people use when they say that "nothing happens in a vacuum" as if anyone believes events happen in complete isolation or without context. Similarly, historians overuse a transition sentence of the type "____ wasn't the only person who . . . " or "____ wasn't the only time that . . . " when no one had actually suggested the contrary.

Poor historical writing also stems from the desire to impress your peers with overly formal, technical language and jargon. Historians who place long, untranslated French or Latin quotes in their text are pretentious, and they alienate their readers. It might be a mark of an eighteenth-century gentleman to read in these languages, but historians today are a much more diverse crowd, with different skill sets. Others consistently employ the term "methodology" when they should write "method." Much of the field of the philosophy of history is laden with postmodern language of the type that wins bad writing contests. And still, without irony, writers in this field complain that other historians don't pay attention to them!

Writing Consistently and Confidently

It is important also to maintain writing efforts when switching jobs, when poor, broke, sick, or injured. This demonstrates an unshakable consistency. There will sometimes be days or weeks when it is truly impossible to find time to write, but making writing a priority limits the frequency of those days. Scholarly productivity is determined by a simple shift in tense. Stop saying, "I *will* write something," and start saying, "I *am* writing something." The truth is, most of the time, only you will know how hard you are working. It is important to write for practice and not to be afraid of roughness of the first draft (or the second draft, or the third draft, etc.). The management of sentences, the use of rhetorical devices, the rhythm of narration, and your own personal tone and style all come in time as you learn the craft of writing. Hours and years of practice will hone your skills.

Although patience and hard work are necessary, each historian must find his or her own way of going about the task. History writing should be an expression of the writer's individuality. There can be no template, no formula or prescription for originality. In my mind, writing is an uncontrollable urge to organize my thoughts and send them on their way. Claude Levi-Strauss had a similar opinion. He said that he would forget his work as soon as it was finished. He poured everything into a topic until he had nothing left to give. Like Levi-Strauss, I want to talk about new research, and not go back over old articles I've written in the past.

Fear, for some people, is the greatest impediment to writing. There is the fear of being outed as a fraud or imposter, the fear of being wrong, and the fear of being mocked and attacked for your views or your inadequacies as a writer. A professor who does not publish is safe from this fear. He or she can always be working on something, or pretending to be, safe in the secret knowledge that the project will never actually see the light of day. For such a person, the consequences of breaking that protective shell are too great.

Most importantly, good writers must learn to overcome rejection. Most scholars acknowledge that hard work is the only path to success, but it can be a struggle to accept that hard work does not necessarily lead to success. In my time, I have written and ultimately abandoned articles on the history of the Florida State Seminole mascot,[9] the development of Virginia's frontier culture history museum,[10] and the migration of Faroese Americans,[11] among other topics. I found all of these topics interesting, or I wouldn't have done the research in the first place. But sometimes a historian can't find enough information to build a relevant interpretation, or maybe there just isn't an audience for the topic.

Prolific researchers respect the sunk-cost fallacy, which is that because you have poured time and money into a project does not mean that you need to see it through to the end. Not everything can or should be published, and it is difficult to know prior to starting research whether you will have anything to say that is worth publishing. Rejection, failure, and quitting are part of academic life. If you do not get turned down from time to time, you are not trying hard enough. If you don't quit something now and then, you will have trouble finding time to move on to new things. Ending one project allows you to start something new, and to try again to convince others of the merits of your ideas. If you retreat after failure, you won't get anywhere. You win zero percent of the grants you don't apply for, you publish none of the articles that you do not submit to journals, and you get into none of the prestigious programs that never receive your application.

In addition to rejection, historians must accept that their peers will criticize them, and that these criticisms may be harsh, personal, and blatantly false, and that despite this all, there might be no good opportunity to respond. Book reviews work this way, for example. Many scholars want to look tough by taking a critical stand against a book for its omissions or errors, but finding no major problems, they dwell on minutiae. Since no book can be exhaustive, reviewers can always criticize a work for failing to cite a particular piece of literature. Chances are, the author of the book is aware of the relevant scholarship but may have chosen not to reference it because they don't think it is worth bringing into the discussion, or because they wanted to save space. Young scholars should recognize that they gain no prestige by writing an overly critical review; they only make an enemy of the author, who may be a future colleague or even a future member of a search committee reading their application. Sometimes, a scholar needs to write an absolutely devastating review, but critics should always strive to be charitable and never nasty.[12]

Creative Writing and Cranks

It is easy to get frustrated with the peer-review system with its anonymous critics and its busy and sometimes distant editors with their near impossible demands. And yet, peer review remains essential as a sorting mechanism to keep weak arguments at bay. As peer reviewers, historians reject unpublishable papers and thereby guard their discipline against bad research and poor argumentation. Journals suffer from academic in-breeding, regional and gender biases, and even innate opposition to radical ideas. But it is still necessary to work within the system to find an audience. Novelty is risky and often in error, so the creative mind is no stranger to social alienation and rejection. It is, however, all too easy to confuse this rejection as a sign of true misunderstood genius. The goal of good history, though, must be to connect to others, in this generation, because if not now, then it will never have an impact. It is possible that some of the best works on history are almost completely unknown and that the only copy of some great argument on some important historical controversy is lying unread on a shelf somewhere. But if the nature of the used book market is any indication, valuable writings do not sit and languish long. Most great works of history eventually find their way to their audience.

There are many historians, however, who believe their own writings are underappreciated masterpieces. Many of these people are cranks. A crank is someone who creates something new but who is unable or unwilling to convince anyone else of the usefulness of his ideas. The term "crank" apparently derives from a pun concerning "a person who cannot be turned." A person is a crank if he or she works outside the normal circles of scholarship, presents views that differ radically from the standard interpretations, and is unable to effectively communicate his or her views, despite attaching deep importance to them. The dream of every crank is, of course, to have their ideas valued and validated by future generations. But since they abhor criticism, they often shrink back into reclusivity. A confident crank, however, does not care what society thinks of him. He is defined by his status as an outsider whose social incompetence prevents him from having his views heard.

For the sake of clarity, let me explain that a crank is quite different from a crackpot. Calling someone a crackpot is referring to the weirdness or eccentricities of a person and their views, while in saying that someone is a crank, you are referring to their stubborn, uncompromising, perhaps pathologically asocial denial of views alternative to their own.[13] The two categories overlap to some degree, but it appears to me that while cranks are likely to be crackpots, crackpots are not always cranks. As a rule, there are more crackpots than cranks in a given society. Neither group has much to do with quacks, who are people who put extreme faith in forms of alternative medicine.

A study of crank historians is useful for recognizing the importance of networking in creative production. In 1902, T.G. Onstot opened his work of Illinois local history with the words "Long ages ago, the worst curse that a good man could wish to befall an enemy was that he were compelled to write a book. We make no apology in appearing before the public as a literary crank."[14] Onstot obviously did not hold his audience in high regard, but imagined that a few like-minded gentlemen would find value in his work. In truth, however, rarely does a person cross the "crank-creative border" (a term I am coining here). Creative historians work on their research in cooperative ways and learn to present their results in understandable forms. They are willing to accept criticisms, consider revisions, and even take an alternative viewpoint if the evidence merits it. But a crank remains a crank if he obsesses about an idea without ever finding an application or relating to his audience. In the 1950s, the grandfather of the modern skeptic movement, Martin Gardiner, defined cranks in a similar way. Gardiner saw them as paranoids with delusions of genius, who work in isolation, criticize others, but don't suffer listening to others' criticisms of their own works.[15] We might also contrast cranks with reasonable people. Despite a parade of examples to the contrary, reasonableness remains an essential characteristic of a good historian. A person might be considered reasonable if they meet the following criteria: 1) They are willing to have a conversation to resolve a conflict, 2) They are willing to admit that there are other views on the matter at hand, and 3) They are able to clearly state the opposing view at hand, even in a way that makes that view potentially attractive. Cranks can do none of the above.

I have some sympathy for cranks because I know what it is like to be unware of, or unable to access, the main channels of professional historical discourse. As a young student in the Midwest, and then as a graduate student at a regional state university in the South, I struggled to locate like-minded scholars or an audience for my research. I had more success, I believe, when I joined informal networks on the American East Coast. It was while working in Virginia, however, that my history department received by mail a copy of a book written by a crank. The book was one of those poorly printed conspiracy jobs running to probably a thousand pages. Most of the faculty laughed about it and they informally voted in the department meeting to dispose of the book. (Had anthropologists been present to study our department as a peculiar tribe, they might have labeled this group behavior as a form of shunning, or ritual rejection of a foreign idea). Now, I don't believe that my colleagues should have taken the book too seriously. There was a good chance that it was utter nonsense and not worth anyone's time. But the response of laughter struck me as quite odd. Here was someone, perhaps mentally disturbed, who had obviously put extensive effort into proving some historical theory. I feel bad that we laughed at a social reject, and that we could not spend time to read the book. Have not all of the great mathematicians been partly mad? Don't all young historians begin their quest for knowledge and acceptance with more curiosity than sense, more confidence than connections? Could there have been some value in at least reading this crank's manuscript?

Few professional historians pay any mind to cranks and the type of fringe history and conspiracy history they typically write. Jason Colavito is one notable exception. Although Colavito was not trained in history per se, he patiently and properly applies the standards of professional historical methods to the claims of fringe history, the type of history that deals with topics that the mainstream would reject: i.e. histories of Atlantis, Bigfoot, the paranormal, and theories of extremely long-distance culture diffusion in the ancient world. Colavito demonstrates the types of logical fallacies that these kinds of historians commit and how they distort or invent evidence. For example, many fringe historians build elaborate theories that attempt to connect disparate pieces of evidence. They assume that if two elements share similar features (like the pyramids of Egypt and the temples of the Maya) that these must be closely related. Fringe historians use the word "proof" when they mean "evidence." I once read a fringe history article in which the author wrote that some historical fact had been "proven to his satisfaction." Of course, historians need to convince others, not just themselves. Fringe historians often fail to recognize how cultural items can travel long distances through trade networks. Believing there is a code to be cracked, they make leap of logic to connect disparate parts.

Conspiracy theorists found in places like AM radio like to tell us to "connect the dots" of historical evidence. The assumption here is that there is only one way to connect the dots. Conspiracy websites claim to have proof of aliens or Bigfoot or the New Jersey devil, when they really just have evidence, and poor evidence at that. Conspiracy theorists seldom balance their evidence or consider the alternative explanations. Those who accept a single conspiracy or fringe history theory are bound to sympathize with others. This is because they sympathize with others whose own fringe views on other subjects have also alienated them from their peers. Conspiracy theory land becomes a place of social castaways, where people simultaneously believe multiple, even contradictory, fringe theories.

To avoid becoming a crank or a conspiracist, a creative historian needs to do a few things. First, she needs to collaborate and communicate with others, not only so that her ideas can spread far and wide, but also so that she can check her ideas against the knowledge of others. To avoid becoming a crank, a historian also needs to be able to give up on a project and move on to something new. If a book or article is never accepted for publication, it's probably because its thesis is incorrect or uninteresting, rather than that it is a misunderstood masterpiece. This is why it is important to be humble and sober. Chances are, you are neither the next David McCullough (often recognized as the United States' leading historian), nor are you a crank with no hope of social acceptance. Chances are, if you have come this far in this book, you are an intelligent, developing historian with real ideas and real potential. You should know then that peer reviewers at major journals are generally reasonable, well-regarded figures in their field. If you send your written work to a journal, you may have to deal with some unwarranted opposition from one set of reviewers, but in that case, you can always send your work to another journal. It is unlikely that you will repeatedly encounter rogue, incompetent, or cruel reviewers.

It seems like a lot of unnecessary work, but maybe the volumes of cranks ought to be read, dissected, and refuted as part of the job of the historian as a disciplinary duty. What better assignment for a class of students than to allow them to read some massive tome of potential historical quackery so that they might root out falsehoods, debate logic, and discuss sources? It is not just the great books of history that teach us how to be historians. It is also the failures that teach us what not to do and which help us reflect on the historian's craft. In crafting this paragraph, I had originally written this line: "To all the cranks who may be reading this, please do not send me your manifesto." Now, having reconsidered, I'd like to revise that statement. To all the cranks who may be reading this, feel free to send me your work. I won't guarantee that I will read it, but I just might give it to my students.

Inputs and Outputs

The major problem for a crank is that he produces a lot of material but has little interaction with people who might temper his views. To develop as a historian, I think you need the proper ratio of input and output of mental activity that comes with healthy social interaction and networking. Inputs consist chiefly of reading books, attending lectures, listening to podcasts, and hearing the views of friends and colleagues. Outputs consist of expressing your views to friends and to colleagues, lecturing and blogging, leading historical tours, or publishing your written thoughts. Good friends and colleagues are essential because they provide the best way for inputs and outputs to balance each other through conversation. Balanced input and output helps develop balanced thoughts.

When the input-output ratio is unbalanced (or when your group of colleagues is nothing but an echo chamber, or the materials you read are piles of hardbound confirmation bias), the product cannot be creative. The over-worked professor who tries to read a lot and teaches a lot of courses has both high input and output, yet he may create little to no original scholarship because he is too occupied for patient, pondering thought. No daydreaming is allowed in a busy life. Others have too much input but not enough oppor-tunity for output. I call this the "lonely curator syndrome" because it strongly affects staff at small museums and historic sites. Symptoms of lonely curator syndrome include a passion for extolling at length the virtues of their museum or historic site. The syndrome expresses itself most clearly in remote museums, when the curator has few visitors. Upon a visit from an academic, perhaps the first to stop by in a year, the curator may feel compelled to relate their entire knowledge of the site and its significance. After all, this curator knows everything about their museum. "The lighthouse was built in 1896," they tell you. "It is 136 feet high." You try to slink away, but they grab you by the upper arm before you can make a start. "There have been ten lighthouse keepers in the history of the lighthouse. The last one retired in 1976 and they never replaced him, but a guy in the village dresses up like one every year for our annual lighthouse days celebration when we offer a 10 percent discount to all." You've stopped listening, but you are pinned by the conversation and it would be socially awkward to try to escape.

The converse of the lonely curator is the overconfident lecturer who does too much teaching and makes no time for input. The overconfident lecturer has no time to learn new things or to think creatively because he is too busy restating his lectures eight times a year. He becomes, over time, only a second handler of ideas. Having reworked the same lecture again and again, he is completely positive that his interpretation of the events is correct. He has not had time to read a book since graduate school, so his understanding of the historiography ends in whatever year he graduated. While the overconfident lecturer can be insufferable, it is reassuring that others are better off. These are the historians who neither read much history nor tell others much about it. They have few inputs or outputs, but for personal or professional reasons, they call themselves historians, history teachers, or history professors. We needn't spend much time describing these folks; they live in ignorant bliss.

To be creative, be prepared to look in new places for history and to connect with others to maintain a proper ratio of inputs and outputs. To write creative history, you either need to find an original subject, or you need to apply a new perspective to an old subject. A few historical topics have been picked apart from every imaginable angle, then reassembled and picked apart again. For instance, there are probably more books about the Pilgrims at Plymouth than there were Pilgrims at Plymouth. There are hundreds of biographies of Abra-ham Lincoln. A new book on Hitler comes out once a week. While these are important historical figures, worthy of biographical treatment, new works on old topics are often redundant. Creative works identify new topics or new angles to be explored. If you think you've invented a new term, like "Margarine-ization" for your thesis on the "History of Obesity and the Margarine-ization of Butter," google the term and see if it is indeed unique. Being creative is doing what others haven't done and taking the risk that you might fail (and potentially become a crank!). You can take a risk and write on unorthodox topics, but you have to find a way to link them back to the major historiographical questions or concerns. It is possible to write a creative history of the Finno-Ugric languages or clambakes in Rhode Island, but neither seems to have the potential to become bestsellers. Above all, however, creative historians are unpredictable, so the next great work of history might be about just about anything.

Notes

1. For an interesting take on why ideas have to come before words, see an article by Sean Rosenthal. https://fee.org/articles/why-a-gilmore-girl-cant-get-a-job/, accessed March 21, 2018.
2. Jeanette Kemp, Susan Legêne, Matthias van Rossum, and Sebas Rümke, *Geschiedenis Schrijven! Wegwijzer voor historici* (Amsterdam, The Netherlands: University of Amsterdam Press, 2016), 10. My translation of the original in Dutch.
3. Henry Glassie, *Passing the Time in Ballymenone* (Bloomington, IN: Indiana University Press), 13.
4. Frank Ankersmit, *History and Tropology: The Rise and Fall of Metaphor* (Berkeley, CA: University of California Press, 1994), 39.
5. Pieter Jan Bouman, *In de Ban der Geschiedenis* (Assen, The Netherlands: Van Gorcum, 1961), 57–58.
6. Michael Munger, "Writing Your Dissertation and Creating Your Research Agenda" in *Scaling the Ivory Tower: The Pursuit of an Academic Career* (Arlington, VA: Institute for Humane Studies, 2005 [original 1995]), 23–24.
7. Italics are original. Walter Carruthers Sellar and Robert Julian Yeatman, *1066 and All That: A Memorable History of England* (New York: E. P. Dutton & Co., Inc., 1953 [original 1931]), vii. The British have a particularly good sense of humor about their history. To help Alice dry out, a mouse in Alice in Wonderland recited the driest thing he knew: a history of William the Conqueror.
8. Kieran Healy, "Fuck Nuance" *Sociological Theory* 35.2 (2017), 118–127. Kieran Healy's "Fuck Nuance" uses a shocking and funny title to press a serious point against the fetishization of complexity in professional sociology.
9. I have good evidence to believe that the Florida State University student election to choose a mascot for the recently co-educational school was rigged by the school's football players, because they believed that the name "Seminoles" was masculine. In 1986, FSU alumnus Bill Bantz recalled that during the election for a school symbol, he and his fellow football players had, in good nature, tampered with the vote:

   > I watched every damn ballot that went through, and a whole lot of 'em that didn't have "Seminole" on them, I threw away. At the time, doctoring these ballots seemed the thing to do. When you played football there then, you were actually bigger than you were, you know, and you could get by with a lot.

   "No Longer the No-Named Team," newspaper clipping from unidentified source. In Linda Carson Lewis, "The Relationship between Florida State University and the Seminole Tribe of Florida." Florida State University Department of Anthropology, Documentation Project, 1999.
10. The Frontier Culture Museum should be one of the major museums in the country, but it has always failed to live up to its promise. Governors who supported

the museum publicly knew they would gain credit for having created something, while leaving their predecessors with no further obligations. A wildly incorrect feasibility study led to unrealistic expectations of revenue. The relative success of local fundraising, as well as the Commonwealth of Virginia's stake in the project, undermined the national direction of the museum. Under the original plan, the museum was to be international, focused on folk culture, with a scholarly component. As the museum struggled, many saw this original vision as impractical. The museum became increasingly focused on the Shenandoah Valley, and tried to diversify its message in order to appeal to a greater segment of the population. Diversification itself became a problem, however, as it alienated significant portions of those who were initially interested in the concept of a museum dedicated narrowly to European-American experience on the frontier.

11. In the United States, Faroese immigrants were too few and too widely scattered to form ethnic organizations, or even to meet accidentally. But networks of extended family bound Faroese Americans to their homeland and to each other. Perhaps no other ethnic group in the United States is as interrelated through kinship, despite such wide dispersion.

12. An illustrative example of a devastating review that leaves out personal attacks is Leonard Dinnerstein's review of Jack Kinton, "American Ethnic Revival: Group Pluralism Entering America's Third Century" *The Journal of American History* 64:4 (March 1978), 1174–1175.

13. Crackpot is also happily a village in North Yorkshire.

14. Thompson Gains Onstot, *Pioneers of Mason and Menard Counties* (Peoria, IL: J.W. Franks & Sons 1902), 13.

15. Martin Gardiner, *Fads & Fallacies in the Name of Science*, 2nd revised edition (Mineola, NY: Dover Publications, 1957 [original 1950]).

6   Networking

The Entrepreneurial Historian

When you think of entrepreneurs, you might think of self-starting business-men like Bill Gates and Steve Jobs—guys who slept in their offices or tinkered in their garages, risking everything for an idea. On the surface, entrepreneur-ship and academia seem like polar opposites. Entrepreneurs find their own paths and take risks in the marketplace. Academics, on the other hand, go to graduate school, often because it's the safe choice when they don't know what else to do. The typical vision of the entrepreneur is of a self-starter with their own, original ideas. In contrast, academics mimic those who came before, repeating the views of their advisors, and, after years of prescribed courses of study, apply for jobs at a set number of colleges and universities.

But I want to suggest that entrepreneurship is actually an essential charac-teristic for academic historians who wish to think creatively. Being a historian requires more skills than reading, writing, lecturing, and learning to patch the elbows of a tweed jacket.[1] Succeeding as a historian requires hustle, hard work, and an entrepreneurial mind.

Entrepreneurial activity is the search for advantages and novelty that will restructure existing orders. One goal of entrepreneurship can be to make money, but it is also to gain autonomy, self-expression, social value, and the enjoyment that comes from working with others. Entrepreneurship for histo-rians is about more than finding ways to make money on the side, or landing a new job through new network connections, although it may be about these things. Entrepreneurial historians are motivated to find new interesting topics to work on for personal satisfaction, and they want to develop new relation-ships by sharing knowledge. It is easy and comfortable to stay in the domain of knowledge you know best. Being an entrepreneur in historical research means always throwing yourself into unfamiliar terrain, humbling yourself and starting anew to work first toward competence, then toward expertise. Entre-preneurial, creative historians are never satisfied with just maintaining their knowledge. Rather, they seek to expand it.

Most discussions of entrepreneurship for historians concern jobs outside of academia, establishing historical research agencies and the like. This is a rather narrow conception of entrepreneurship as an alternative to traditional careers in academia. For most historians, it would be very difficult to survive as a freelance writer or historical consultant. It is also quite difficult to establish your own research associate firm. But entrepreneurship for historians should be conceived of in broader terms, not as a tool for creating an alternative career or finding side employment, but as a general outlook towards knowledge.

Entrepreneurial, creative historians do not need to have full-time jobs as history professors or researchers. For my own part, I direct an institute in a business school, and do my historical research on the side. There really is no limit to what career you can have while still thinking and working as a historian in your free time. One might work a regular 9-to-5 job and still be a historian on the side. Maintaining personal ties to an academic faculty or holding a university staff position of some sort, however, is useful to gain library access, meet interesting colleagues, and gain status in the academic world. A teaching or research job is a privilege for those interested in ideas. But better-paying jobs are more easily found outside of academia than inside it.

The entrepreneurial mindset is important for historians who want to continue creative work despite dropping out of academia. Today's job market is a difficult place for professional historians, and I see many history graduate students essentially give up on their historical research when they are unable to find a faculty position as a history professor. If the perfect position is not given to them within a year or two of graduation, they consider alternative careers, and when they find these other careers, they generally stop historical research and writing altogether. This demonstrates to me that many graduate students in history do not really want to be historians in the first place. They enjoy being students, competing for prestige, and writing the occasional article. But without the support structure around them, without grants and assistantships and encouragement from their professors, they conduct little or no research.

Where, Why, and How to Network ✓✓

A key aspect of entrepreneurship is networking. Networking is crucial for creative historical thinking because it is an efficient way to find new knowledge. For many historians, networking is a neglected skill. It can be uncomfortable. We prefer to think that we will make it on our own and that the merit of our work will be enough. But more often than not, the spoils of academia, particularly well-placed academic jobs, go to those who are well connected. While some of this bias towards connected scholars is plain old nepotism, much of it is a form of justifiable discrimination if we consider that connected scholars are likely to be better informed and more personable colleagues. Historians might struggle with social skills, but history is a social discipline. What is new is sometimes uncomfortable, and what is comfortable is usually not new, but when we force ourselves to get outside of our comfort zone and network with others, we discover our own limitations and realize new potential.

For many years, I was a hedgehog of a historian; I never came out of my office. I figured networking was a waste of time and that I would succeed through publishing articles in top journals. But this started to change when I got my first teaching job and had the opportunity to get business cards. I handed these cards out like candy. I gave them to my colleagues, to members of the community, and to scholars I met at conferences. By the end of the year, this had led to all kinds of invitations, speaking opportunities, and friendships. I was surprised when one colleague responded by saying that he had never had business cards made because he couldn't imagine any situation in which he would give them out. This colleague taught public history classes, the very courses that teach history students how to engage with the public.

Some people might be discouraged from networking because they don't see immediate benefits. But networking is a long-term strategy, with dividends that come years later. Many links in a social network will lie dormant for years. A lot of people you meet you will never see again, and even though they have your business card, they will never think of contacting you. But some will. And when you have a skill or some expertise to offer, knowledge of this will spread through the grapevine. Someone you connected to years ago may alert you to a new primary source or a new book. If you respond each time, making yourself available and never closing yourself off, you will become known as a responsible, responsive historian. Once the channels of communication are formed, knowledge and connections will flow to you. At first, you may accept some work without pay, but learn to recognize when you should be paid for your work. Things like reviewing books, answering emails about historical questions, and writing op-eds are simply part of the profession and you should not demand or expect compensation for this kind of work. However, if you provide long translations, give invited lectures, or conduct research for another person, you should expect to be compensated. Again, there is no fast rule here, but you do gain respect of others by establishing that your time has value.

Certainly, one should network within historians' circles, but it also pays to network with scholars from other disciplines. From the vantage point of our own discipline, the whole world can make perfect sense. It is easy to think then that everyone else in other disciplines is either doing some inferior kind of work, or nothing of any particular value. The less knowledge we have about a subject, the less likely we are to see the fine distinctions between scholars and their writings. So, someone who does not study economics might crudely think that all economists just study money and wealth, and not human action more generally. Many historians are jealous of the power of the economics profession, but their hatred of economics is usually proportional to their ignorance of it. Because historians tend to be broadly historicist, they might dismiss economic theory not on the grounds of the coherence or incoherence of its internal logic, but because it does not line up with their understanding of empirical evidence. When the evidence doesn't match the theory, it gives us cause for doubt. Historians might also think sociologists are unredeemable "lumpers" who just propose unreasonably general categories for human behavior. On further inspection, however, sociological theory might provide an explanation for a perplexing historical phenomenon.

Fortunately, this scholarly cooperation works in both directions, and historians have much to offer scholars in other fields. Whether it is economics, linguistics, or law, a historian might enter these fields to provide some big-picture perspective on developments over time. While scholars in these fields are thinking synchronically—that is, considering a subject outside of time—a historian can look at the subject diachronically, embedded in the flow of time. While many scholars have grudges against businessmen, economists, lawyers, and other professionals, no one seems to hate historians by default. What this means is that historians are generally well-liked, or at least tolerated, and can easily slip into new crowds of scholars without arising too much suspicion of their motives.

Entrepreneurship is more than coming up with inventions, seeking capital, and taking on risk. Entrepreneurship is also the creativity to consider new arrangements. When you work outside of your field, you bring in skills that others may not have. When you network outside of your field, you bring in skills that others are looking for. Many historians think that their discipline does not have a valuable set of skills to offer others. But this is completely mistaken. The research skills and writing abilities that historians often take for granted can be valuable currency in legal studies, sociology, economics, or other social science disciplines. Knowledge that one discipline takes for granted might be entirely new in another, and skills that are common in one field might be quite rare in another. If you are willing to be the bridge between disciplines and humble yourself to what you don't know, you may discover that disciplines can be having simultaneous, parallel conversations on the same topic. Each discipline may have a piece of the puzzle, or a limited view of the whole. Recognizing and taking advantage of opportunities for cooperation is priceless.

My point is that history is an ecumenical discipline. A historian marching into territory covered by political science, ethics, or other normative disciplines finds it is easy to play the role of an outside agnostic in those disciplines' great debates. In this way, historians can contribute something for all to hear without alienating rival camps. By writing hybrid articles that combine two or more disciplines, you can rightly claim to be doing multidisciplinary or interdisciplinary work. When you can no longer tell what field you are in, you can begin to write about topics that are of general interest. A philosophy professor from Oxford once told me not to worry if I was not always working in one field. Instead of majoring in history or philosophy, for example, he said, it was better to just "major in thinking." I couldn't help thinking of the scarecrow in the Wizard of Oz, who receives from the wizard a diploma with the honorary degree of "Th.D.": Doctor of Thinkology. Ideally, we should all be "thinkologists."

While many academics disparage overly theoretical or ideological disciplines, history has the benefit of being rather neutral on the whole. This is because historians concentrate more on content than on theories, and while they certainly are motivated by theories and ideologies, they are somewhat less likely to broadcast these as explicitly as do scholars in, say, economics or sociology. Historians are hedgehogs and curmudgeons, who focus narrowly on evidence from one time and place. As a result, they sometimes have trouble speaking with people working on widely different topics, or fields of history. What can an Americanist learn from a historian of Mongolia? they might think. Or what can a modern historian learn by reading about the kings of medieval Europe? Within our subfields and specializations, we are confident, often to the point of being too argumentative, or holding grudges against other historians who work on the same topic but hold views that depart from ours in the smallest ways. On the whole, however, it seems that historians are less argumentative by nature than are scholars in other disciplines like philosophy, economics, or political science, where competing theories and interpretations can and are applied across various datasets.

In networking, you don't need to pose as an expert. Instead, make it clear that you don't have all the answers but would be glad to work with someone to figure them out. Praise others who tell you new things, and listen patiently when someone tells you a story that you have already heard. Maybe there are new elements of the story in this new version. Real work is being done during face-to-face conversations and between class periods and conference presentations. Networking can be done online, but it is the in-person interactions that people remember.

Ideas for Networking

Opportunities for networking are all around you. Help young and old, big and small, with their questions about history. One way to start gaining skills as a historian is to help others with genealogical research. Genealogy can be the bane of historians if they don't respect it. I still remember the day, back when I was an intern at a museum library in Massachusetts, when a patron came in to ask for genealogy help. The archival librarian on staff appeared unnaturally red-faced, huffing and puffing, as he stepped out of his office. I asked what was wrong. He looked at me with a frown, put his hand on the top of his head, and exclaimed, "I HATE genealogists!" Instead of getting frustrated, a better option is to offer a few minutes of help. You don't have to do all of the research for someone. Just give them a few pointers and lead them on their way. Through genealogical research, you learn about family naming patterns, migration patterns, and changes in tax and household laws, and so on. Genealogical knowledge can seem too specific to be of much use to an old-fashioned historian of grand ideas, but its cumulative lessons contribute to a historian's overall knowledge. Helping others connect with their family's past can be a rewarding learning experience.

If you want to become a creative historian, just look around you for inspiration. Tell people in your community that you are interested in local history, and you will be invited to visit old buildings and listen to old people tell stories. Volunteer to give a presentation at a local high school, and the history teacher there will be happy to be relieved of an hour of planned lessons. Join the local historical society. As someone who has moved often in my adult life,

I have found it easy to play the role of the new person in town, an outsider who wishes to know more about the area he has moved to. Most people are eager to tell their own stories and relate the stories of their neighborhoods. A key here, especially if you are new to the area, is that you must not present yourself as an expert who has come to take over. Don't criticize members of the society. Ask questions and be eager to listen. You will learn more that way. Once you have established yourself in the group, you might be invited to look at local historical sites, help identify locally found artifacts, or serve as a judge at local school history fair.

Tell your neighbors that you are a historian and they might bring you stories or pieces of local history. Earlier this year, a neighbor brought me a collection of fifteen letters that he said he had found in an old log cabin years ago. He didn't know what they were about or where they came from. We sat down together to read through the letters. We built up a story from the sources. Most of the letters dated to the 1890s and documented a relationship. The early ones were between Andrew Scanlon and Mollie Smith. In the later letters, the name Mrs. Mollie Scanlon appears. Eureka, they were love letters!

This find and this reading exercise did not lead to any major revision in historical knowledge. But if you are always looking for the smoking gun or the X that marks the spot, you are doing history wrong. Historical knowledge is built piece by piece or by small steps. The more you engage with historical sources, the more you strengthen your ability to analyze sources. Each time I encounter new sources, I get to hang new facts on my mental timeline. My mental image of a particular time and place comes into focus slowly. Because I have spent many hours in archives reading old letters, I could tell my neighbors things about the Scanlon letters that they would not have known themselves. I could tell them, for example, something about the age of the paper and its qualities. I could tell them about the days before rural free delivery and a bit about the history of stamps and the postal service.

To network among other academics, go to history conferences specifically to make connections, not just to get a line on your CV. In my experience, there are many historians with poor social skills, and many of them at conferences just sit alone at the bar, waiting for someone to talk to. Break the ice, ask a question about history, and you might have just made a new colleague. If you attend a conference or a seminar in a discipline outside your own, you are likely to gain more new ideas, and find ways to connect to knowledge outside of your field. When you meet people at conferences, it can lead to invitations to other events, possible co-authorship opportunities, reference letters, and more.

Perhaps the most important networking tool is your own website, with a blog about your ideas on history. Keeping a history blog will allow you to practice writing. You can post short-form articles about history books that you have read, artifacts that you have found, and views that you have developed. A blog can showcase a specific interest or serve as an eclectic mix of what you are interested in. With consistent effort, the blog might attract readers and opportunities. It also makes you a known entity, a person whom others can find and invite to events. A blog is useful because when people type in specific terms (particularly certain historical names), they will find your work. A website is useful to advertise your books and articles, to announce that you are available to give presentations, review historical materials, or consult on history projects. You can create links to other history blogs and encourage reciprocation.

A personal website works in combination with all of the rest of what you publish and do. In my current position directing a research institute, I often recruit graduate students for seminars and conferences. I might hear of a bright, interesting student to invite to one of our events, but if I can find no information about that person online (no CV, no personal blog, no publications available online), I am not likely to get in touch with them. If you do not exist online, you are limiting your possible network. Increasingly, there are foundations, institutions, and research centers of all kinds that are expanding their seminar schedules and looking for interesting people to invite into their networks. If you email them and express your interest in what they do, you will be more likely to receive an invitation to participate in one of their programs. You might begin as a student of whatever it is that they study, and in the long run, you might get paid to teach the same. Network connections cost some time and energy to build. It might even cost money to attend events in these networks; but if done right, the opportunities that arise will outweigh the costs. I might be wrong, but as far as I know, no graduate programs in history are teaching their students how to make personal webpages. This is a serious gap in historical education, because historians gain immensely by using social networking sites, obviously for connecting to friends and colleagues on Facebook, but also to find jobs and present their work through sites like LinkedIn, academia.edu, the Social Science Research Network, ResearchGate, and personal websites. No longer do we need to subscribe to the journals and magazines, but we receive information more quickly. We learn about new trends sooner. Today's prevailing metaphor of history is a hyperlinked "web" of events and people. For the entrepreneurial historian, the takeaway is obvious: If you are not connected, you are at a massive disadvantage. You're either digital, or you're dead.

The most important advice I can give about networking as a historian is to express your thanks. Be the person who sends a thank-you letter to your hosts after you are invited to speak at a seminar or conference. If you appreciated being invited to seminars or being allowed to participate in projects, let people know. Even if this does not lead immediately to more opportunities, you will build a good reputation. Staying in touch with a few words takes only a few seconds, but it keeps you on the minds of others for future projects and invitations.

Entrepreneurship can be exhausting, and there are physical and mental demands on the working historians. Long hours traveling, lecturing, and researching is not equivalent to digging in the salt mines, but there is a share of drudgery in photographing a thousand leaves of an old book or keystroking thousands of lines while compiling a database. There is the stress of dealing with stern archivists in foreign languages, and patience required when someone you meet tries to impress you with one of the trite old lines about your field:

"Learn history or you are bound to repeat it," "history is only written by the winners," and so on.

Cooperation

In a famous article titled "I, Pencil," Leonard Read explained that no single person on earth could make a pencil.[2] He explained that thousands of people are needed to produce pencils. There are tree harvesters, for example, and people who mine pyrite. There are glue makers, rubber tree cultivators, paint suppliers, and hundreds of middlemen. In the same way, a history article may be assembled by one person, but it requires the cooperation of many more. Although history articles or books might have a single author, they cannot be written without the contribution of hundreds, if not thousands, of people. History is a cooperative discipline, and creative historians must work with others.

If a historian goes by herself to an archive to get newspaper articles for her research, she may sit alone in the reading room, but her research is supported by many others. First, there were the front-line witnesses to the past and those who recorded the moment or collected and stored pieces of evidence. This includes people at the scene of an event, journalists who interviewed those people, newspaper editors who sent the journalists' articles to print, and myriad others, including copyeditors, typesetters, printers, and newspaper carriers. Subscribers preserved news clippings in shoeboxes or albums, and the newspaper editor kept old papers on file at his office. At some point, a microfilm company sent an agent along to make a copy of those stacks of newspapers, and the microfilm was then processed and sent to libraries. The physical papers were brought to an archive, where they were labeled and cataloged by an archivist. And then, years later, an archival assistant retrieved the item for the researcher. Each source available to a historian was, at some point, selected from all possible remains of the past. The source was preserved (by a person, or by nature), or replicated. At some point, the source was uncovered, retrieved, or brought back into mind.

Of course, every work of historical research should cite interpretations from other historians who have written on the topic. Honest historians recognize their humble status when they write that they merely "stand on the shoulders of giants," or that they have only contributed another brick to the foundation that previous historians had built. No historian starts from scratch, then. Rather, historians are able to survey vast historical terrain relatively quickly, relying on the power of the division of labor and the work that others have done to scan, interpret, and summarize various parts of the past. Any given history article has contributions from a census taker, a journalist, a record keeper, and a web designer who built the site where the historical information was accessed.

The innumerable, anonymous inventions and creative acts accumulate from the experiences of many. From this perspective, all of human culture is the result of creative thinking. When we read the work of other historians, our minds work through the same historical problems they do, and our moments of insight come from understanding the connections they make. Reading great works, we feel that we are ourselves being creative, and we share in the pleasure of discovery of the inferences that are new to our minds.

In history, as in nearly any discipline, creativity is a cooperative enterprise. Historians are less likely to co-author an article than are a group of scientists, but historical work never develops in complete isolation. Historians always take into consideration the views of other writers on the topic. Partly for this reason, and because it takes time to locate evidence, creativity in history develops slowly, and seldom does a great historian emerge at an early age. Historical interpretation tends not to experience the sorts of sudden and radical bursts of progress that can happen in the sciences, nor does it quickly lead to high citation counts and jobs at top institutions. Writing creatively is a function of social atmosphere, and cooperation and interaction with others, and the reward—beyond your own personal satisfaction, and perhaps a decent teaching job—comes over the long term, as your views slowly work their way into the mainstream. The Dutch historiographical tradition speaks of history as a "discussion without end." This is, I think, a fascinating metaphor for history, and one that is not used often in an American context. History is a discussion between the present and the past, and between people in the present. Each work of history contributes to the discussion. If we conceive of history in such a way, we can read along with the poet Walt Whitman: "The powerful play goes on, and you may contribute a verse!"[3]

Notes

1. This may be an actual course at certain Ivy League schools. I'm not sure.
2. Leonard Reed, "I, Pencil: My Family Tree as Told to Leonard E. Read" *The Freeman* (May 1966).
3. Walt Whitman, "Leaves of Grass," 1855 (Philadelphia, PA: D. McKay, 1883 [original published, New York, 1855]), 215.

7 My Backyard History Chapter

If you buy a house, you will learn the history of your property bit by bit, whether you want to or not. While moving in to the house, for example, you might find an old key hidden behind a pantry door or an old photograph on the top shelf of a built-in bookcase. A few weeks later, when your faucet springs a leak, you might discover to your dismay that a water pipe has been installed improperly. Ten years on, and your house has the potential to still yield some secrets of its past. Small signs of past inhabitants include the remnants of a tennis ball behind a bush in the backyard, letters in a box hidden in the attic, or messages scrawled beneath now-covered surfaces. All of these things around the house come together to tell you something about the life of the previous occupants. In this chapter, I present the story of my own search for the history of my property. Through this, I discuss some creative strategies for learning about the history of your own home. Owning a home can be a rewarding long-term history project.

In owning a home, historical knowledge of the place has real practical value, especially for home improvement concerns. Usually, you will only get one chance to speak with the past owners, so my advice is to not neglect to ask them questions about the history of the property. In fact, you should grab them by the arm and keep them as long as they can stand it. Every minute interviewing the former owners can save hours of trouble or confusion down the line. How does the heater work? Who did the wiring in the house? Where did the materials come from? If you ever want to match material and patch damage to the house, you might want to know if stones came from the river down the road, or a state away. If you live on an older property, you might ask about previous structures. Was there ever another house on site, or any outbuildings that you might discover one day when you ruin your lawnmower blades against the protrusion of an old foundation stone?

A little over a year ago, I bought a house in the mountains of West Virginia, in Hampshire County, the oldest and largest county in the state. Along with a house dating to 1986, I acquired an "old" barn of indiscriminate age, two chicken coops, and a modern metal shed. Although the previous inhabitants had moved out most of their personal possessions, I found that I had plenty of stuff left behind that needed sorting through. From the past owners, I learned a bit about the history of the place. An old, unused road in the woods—a road which they called "the Braddock Road"—formed the edge of my property. I was taught how to work the indoor stove and the outdoor stove. I heard stories about the old man who built the house as a retirement cabin the 1980s. I was given the names of some old neighbors who knew more about the area. I held on to the phone number of the past owner in case I had any pressing concerns. I didn't want to bother him once he moved on, but it would be insurance if I ever found anything that needed explaining.

Then, after a good one-hour conversation, the former owner drove off and I was left alone to figure out the rest. It is at this point that a historian gains sympathy for the existentialists, if he does not already count himself one of them. We are all faced with the problem of finding meaning in the world around us, and we start by acquiring information through the senses. There is a dread of not knowing the meaning of it all, and a profound freedom to act in whatever way we think best for learning. I could have just sat inside all through that first cold fall and winter, reading Sartre and Camus, but I decided instead to get busy on the property. I wanted to improve the property—but more so, I wanted to understand it.

In the fall of 2016, I began my historical adventure in the barn, where I spent most of my energy for the first half year. The barn was standing, and most of the beams were in good shape. One side of the barn needed serious attention, however. The beams there looked like they had been repaired or reinforced in the past decade, but whether they would last the winter, I wasn't entirely sure. I half-expected to wake up after a big snowfall with a barn half caved-in. I remembered the sketches in those old Eric Sloane books, where Sloane explains that snow is the major culprit of roof collapse. When a roof is gone, the building will deteriorate at a much faster pace. The freeze-thaw cycle causes old nails in wood boards to rise at a very slow rate, perhaps a millimeter per decade. But, over time, the nails will lose their grip. The barn clearing needed a new roof, with new nails. Every time I would mow the grass or just walk around the barn, I'd find another few pieces of tar paper shingles in the grass. This was a ticking clock, a warning that soon enough there would be no more tar paper left and roof would open up to the sky and the barn would inevitably rot from the inside out, caving in for a final death.

The first problem with my barn was that it was full of modern trash. While there was no noticeable smell of rot or mold, bags of trash filled the barn knee-deep. These bags, it turned out, obscured piles of valuable hardwoods, much of which had rotted, but a good deal remained that was salvageable, and would later become flooring in the house, siding for a new shed, and various things like wooden checkerboards and custom doorstops. Most of it, however, became firewood that first winter, as I wheel-barrowed load after load of warped, rotten, and nail-filled lumber from the barn to the outdoor wood stove. I've heard that there is money in old barn wood, but the truth is, the wood has to be nearly nail-free, straight and in good condition. To sell it, you have to clean the wood, remove any nails, stack it, and wait. If you find a buyer willing to come out to pick it up, you might profit. But in the long run, all that work might not be worth it, and you're better off using the wood for your own projects.

A Diary of a Barn

That fall, as I began to learn about the history of the barn, I also started writing a diary of my efforts to clean it out, repair it, and understand what had gone on there. My first entry reads:

> October 24, 2016. I've scythed the grass around the chicken coop, uncovering it and its neighbor building. The barn is an archaeologist's task. In the barn's office, I discovered signs of relatively recent habitation . . . a 1990 newspaper from Romney, WV, and a 1963–1966 Encyclopedia Britannica yearbook.

Three days later, I was excited to learn more, and angry to find more trash under a pile of wood.

> October 27, 2016. There are dates inscribed on the door: 1913 is the oldest. A beam on the inside appears to read "80", but is worn beyond the point of legibility. Yesterday, I burned a large pile near the barn. Turns out it was more than just the pinewood scrap on top, but a dump, including a cast-off dishwasher.

In the months to follow, I found other dump sites on the property. Household dumps were and unfortunately still are common in West Virginia. Many of these date to the early twentieth century, when Americans started to eat canned goods. The first few cans a family acquired could be put to use as receptacles for holding nails or other supplies. After a while, though, each additional can became less valuable on the margin. Tin cans, along with glass and some shattered pottery, seem to make up the bulk of the material in household dumps in the region.

When I was cleaning out the barn, I was still referring to the barn's granary as an "office," since I didn't know better. The granary was the only room in the barn that could be closed off entirely behind a door and latch. This meant it was a room where the detritus of the past could hide out and survive. A few weeks later in the fall, I spent an afternoon at work in the granary/office:

> November 16, 2016. I've cleaned out the office. It was full of old chairs, windows, doors, lady bugs, spider webs, wasps' nests, and dirt. I've created a small "collection of old metal barn tools" on display on the main table in the center of the barn. There is still a lot of wood and materials to sort through, to sell or give away, to dump or burn. A few days ago I carved "MJD 2016" into the door of the barn office. It stands beside inscriptions from 1913, 1980, and 2010.

This may have been the first time in my life that I carved my initials into anything. I am generally against the practice just because I don't like to see things all marked and pocked, especially at public sites. But I also appreciate historic inscriptions and believe they are a largely unexplored source of information about the past. I once wrote but never published a paper on historic inscriptions in the Shenandoah Valley.[1] Carving my initials to the door, I established a tangible link to the property and to a tradition. I felt that I was now the keeper of the structure, a 30×40-foot, two-and-half-story wooden box dating to the late nineteenth century. My goal was not to restore it to its original look or use, since both would be impossible. Instead, I hoped to clean it out and make it usable again, maybe as a woodworking shop or at least as an organized storage space. In time, I learned the names of all of the abbreviations carved on the barn. I knew who "JES" was when he carved his initials in 1980, and who "AES" was when he carved his in 1923.

As I shoveled out old piles of corn and manure, and tore out rotten boards of old horse stalls, I found artifacts of various age, indicating previous activities on the site.

> December 10, 2016. I've done a lot of work over the past few weeks. With a crow bar and rubber hammer, I have knocked out corncribs and horse stalls. I have been hauling rotten boards, misshaped boards, etc., to the house, where I have set up a miter saw on a table. I then cut the boards, and return them to be stacked neatly in the barn. There is a lot of hydrated lime laying around, but I've managed to stay upwind of it while I work. I found a 19th century carpenter's axe snugly jammed between some boards in the horse stall. I have also found a lot of glass, various metal objects, leather, etc. There is hay and corn. Today, I found a pair of nearly mint condition spectacles in the style of Theodore Roosevelt. I also found another carving on a board. It is difficult to read.

The old pair of glasses, still with a sticker reading "13" (perhaps a prescription number) on the lens, was far and away my favorite find in all those hours of shoveling and pitch-forking out the old manure and hay from the barn. The glasses were perfectly preserved in a closed metal case, with purple velvet on the inside. I also found a small green plastic toy plane the size of a quarter, and shop-worn chrome "football man" missing his feet, likely the remaining part of a football trophy.

Oral Memory

When I had come close to cleaning out the barn, disposing of the waste, and sorting through all that I had found that might be of value, I happened to link into another local source of information on the way. In my diary, I wrote:

> April 30, 2017. Yesterday, I stopped at a yard sale about a mile from where I live. There was nothing I wanted to buy (although I discovered that it is legal to sell guns at yard sales in West Virginia!). Anyway, I introduced myself as a new neighbor from down the way, and explained that I had purchased land

from a particular family. An 80-year old woman sitting nearby looked over at me and said "Oh honey, I was born on that property before electricity came through these parts." So, naturally, as a historian, I responded "Oh reeeee-aaaally?" and asked if I could sit in the lawn chair next to her. For an hour, she told me about milking a cow in my barn, hoeing the cornfields next door, and living in a one-room milkhouse on the property, about how her side of the family lost the property in an inheritance dispute. This Tuesday, the 80-year old lady and her older brother are coming over for a visit. She was so excited on the phone just now. It's just the "darndest thing, honey" she said in the most excited-est cadence I've ever heard.

The visit from the two octogenarians helped me fill in much of the history of the property in the twentieth century. My barn, I learned, was used for grain storage and to hold horses and an automobile. The barn belonged to a house that no longer exists, on what is now my neighbor's land.

The story my guests told was enlightening. They spoke of the house as a "hotel," but its actual size and shape they couldn't describe, since it burned down in the 1920s, a decade before they were born. From the stories of their parents, however, they knew that the hotel had a wrap-around porch, a tele-phone line, and a front door that opened towards the old defunct road in the woods. In the decade after the house burned down, their parents moved into the old milkhouse, a one-room storage building next door that had been spared by the flames. The children grew up in the one-room house, with an additional lean-to room added on, while they hoed the fields and shucked corn in the barn. Life was rough, but free. The family grew corn, apples, pota-toes, and cucumbers. There was no electricity until the 1940s, so the family kept food preserved underground, or in jugs in the cold creek. A spring at the bottom of the driveway provided water for many in the area. Their father had a Model A roadster that would cut its way through the snow. The driveway, my driveway, used to be cut deeper, with higher banks, and it was more or less in the same place, maybe a bit to the left.

I can now walk around my yard on a quiet afternoon with all of these images on my mind. Life is more interesting, the surroundings more colorful, when you know the history of a place.

County Archives

I continued to learn about my property through visits to the county court-house. There, I found records of the property back to the mid-nineteenth cen-tury. It was called "The Mountain Tract" when, on March 15, 1879, the heirs of Robert M. Powell deeded the land to an Arthur L. White.

Besides a flurry of recent modern sales, deeds showed a sale of the property in 1978 and then, going back, 1973, 1922, 1907, 1879, and 1860. All the while, however, the property shifted in shape. My 5-acre parcel was part of a 120-acre farm in the 1970s, but this farm was of various sizes, and may have even moved amoeba-like from one place to another. The thing is, I learned, the land was never mapped in detail before 1978. In the nineteenth century, property in West Virginia was still demarcated by "metes and bounds," the language of "from the two large Oak trees to the Hickory along the ridge"—which was an efficient way of doing things then, but which is almost useless now. Property then was defined also by relation to other land claims, and borders of property were known and negotiated between respective owners.

The oral memory of my property went back to around 1900, to the Sunderlins, and to the Whites, but the name Powell, while prominent in the area, was no longer connected in memory to the site. With archival research, then, I could go further than the community's memory, back probably as far as the 1830s, when Robert M. Powell was purchasing various tracts of land in the area. Then the trail fades out with unclear and incomplete land records from the period. Ultimately, the land was owned by Lord Fairfax as part of his father's land grant from the King of England. I haven't found any projectile points that show a Native American presence, but the relatively high ground with a spring on the site was sure to have lured people to the site long ago.

Metal Detecting

Then, at some point, when you've turned over every rock, spoken to all the neighbors, and flipped through documents at the courthouse, you think that you've exhausted the trail. I had no experience with metal detecting, but it turned out to be a good way to learn more about my land.

Both in the barn and in the yard, I became an amateur archeologist. Archeologists and historians sometimes have competing aims, and I liken some archeologists to archivists in the sense that they are as concerned with preserving things as they are in learning things. I have been warned by archeologists never to encourage anyone to dig who is not trained, and who does not use a professional grid to mark the locations of their discoveries. I'd like to push back, however, against the oppressive, even elitist, attitude of some historical archeologists. Certainly, it would be best if a professional came to my property and marked all of my discoveries along the way. But this is just not practical. If I find a mastodon bone, I'll certainly stop digging. But if I am digging up bottle caps and bullet shells in my front yard, or pottery in the garden, it hardly merits professional attention.

I posted a query in an online metal detecting forum. I pretended to be completely ignorant of the subject, and asked whether it was common to pay someone to detect on a property, or if they would come for free. I had a half-dozen responses within the day. The opportunity to detect on a new property, even with the agreement that they could keep nothing they found, was exciting news for these folks. In the end, I found one of the responses was from a local, a man who lived only 10 miles away. He came for a visit a few weeks later, and returned again a few weeks after that. In total, he visited my property three times, and we made new discoveries each time.

Most metal detecting finds result in little of monetary value. Mostly we found rusty nails, bottle caps and bullet fragments, most of fairly recent date.

We searched the old Braddock Road in the woods and found a rearview mirror from a 1950s automobile, signaling that the old dirt road might have still been accessible to cars at that late date. Alternatively, of course, the mirror was simply discarded by someone living on an adjacent property. At any rate, the road was filled with metal fragments, and nearly all of it was rusty wire that was in some places still visible above ground, strung through hardy black locust posts. At the end of the fence line was a larger post, made from an old beam from a log cabin or perhaps a barn.

Around the barn, we found an old wrench, some minor car and radio parts, pull tabs and caps for milk jugs and beer bottles. We found one coin: a 1966 dime with Franklin Roosevelt on it (before Eisenhower was on the dime). In total, we surveyed only a small percentage of my 5 acres, and there are perhaps many more artifacts to be picked out of the soil.

But through metal detecting, you start to think differently about the land. If you can locate an outhouse, you should detect along the route from the house to the outhouse. If there is an old tree, it is possible that someone once rested up against it and had some change spill out of their pockets. The paths on your property are streams of potential finds.

Signs of the Past

As the year went by, I continued to discover signs of the past around the home. When the pond next door dried up over the summer, I found two cut rectangular stones, what might have been cornerstones from the old "hotel," I figured. I weighed them at over 150 pounds apiece. Elsewhere on the property, especially near property markers, I found similar stones. The thing is, even nicely cut foundation stones take on new purpose when a house burns down. I imagine that these heavy stones migrated around the property from decade to decade as they were put to use in various applications. It was likely not until my property was surveyed in 1978 that stones and metal bars were placed in the corners of the property. Lacking any written sources or standing structures, boundary stones and survey markers would be important sources for an archeologist interpreting a site.

Inside the house, there were signs of the past, as well. When I renovated rooms in the house I found carpenter's mark—not the old roman numerals scratched into barn beams—but pennies left in the walls and under the floorboards. These pennies, I quickly realized, indicated the dates of construction or previous renovation. When I could remember to do so, I followed the tradition and scrounged through my change for pennies with the date 2016 or 2017. When I moved in, I couldn't recognize half of the tools and building materials in the shed. As the year went by, I would encounter a problem in the house and discover that my solution was a tool that I already had in the shed. For example, I found a chimney sweeper, boxes of drywall screws, and clay tiles that matched those in the bathroom. It seemed as if all of the materials I needed for repair were already on hand. In the barn loft, there was house siding to spare.

Other discoveries were equally unexpected. One day, when walking through my woods, I found a weathered wooden cane caught on the branch of a tree. It had been ten years since an old man had lived on the property. I wondered if the cane really could have been hanging on the tree for ten years. I half-expected to find a Tin Man, with his mouth rusted shut and his axe caught in a tree.

There are hidden historical discoveries I look forward to making, but cannot anticipate. For example, after I cut trees and cleared a field to expand the size of my grass-covered front yard, I started to split some of the wood from that section of my property. When I counted growth rings of the trees I had cut, I found that most had around twenty-six rings. The growth of trees in this one area corresponded to a sale of the property twenty-six years ago, when saplings took over a field that was no longer plowed or mowed.

I don't know whether my future historical discoveries about the history of my property will come through digging, flipping through papers, asking questions of neighbors, or by simply turning over another rock, another tree, another board. But I do know that the history I find around my house can inform my lectures in the classroom, can help me understand architectural and cultural history better, and can help me relate better to those in my community who have strong knowledge of the history and practice of home construction. There are architectural histories of homes, and some histories about how people have occupied residential spaces, but given how much of the past has taken place at home, it is a wonder that more history is not written about our most immediate surroundings.

I have begun a house history book. Like an eighteenth-century commonplace book or a twentieth-century scrapbook, it is a collection of all information about my house, including a floorplan sketch that I found, a guide to how to work the outdoor wood stove, a collection of deeds of sale, a record of when certain rooms were renovated or appliances were purchased, and many other things. This house history book includes pictures, stories, data on mortgage payments, and electric bills. If I move, I intend to make a copy for myself, and leave a copy for the new owner, who will certainly benefit from it in many ways.

Note

1. I define historic inscriptions as a cultural product of a literate people, texts and signs engraved or written on *in situ*, nontransportable objects in publicly accessible places. Historic inscriptions may bear similarities to signatures in books and on legal documents, or to makers' marks engraved on pottery and the like, but they cannot be owned in the same sense without destroying their original context. Historic inscriptions can be considered graffiti, a word from the Italian for "to scratch." In an American context, however, "graffiti" commonly refers to the illicit spray-painted markings that first became popular in urban areas in the 1960s. Historic inscriptions in American culture can be dated to the earliest explorers, but they became popular with the rise of literacy and the increased movement of common people in the nineteenth century.

Section III

Creativity in the History Classroom

Section III, consisting of Chapters 8, 9, and 10, deals specifically with strategies for creativity in the classroom. Sooner or later, all historians become teachers of one kind or another, either formally in the classroom, or just in the course of everyday casual conversation. It is important then to learn how to transfer historical information in multiple ways and formats to appeal to various audiences.

History courses usually consist of a mixture of lectures, discussion of assigned readings, and exams. The idea is that a teacher presents information, students read more information, and then they all get together and talk about it. In the end, students recall information for a grade. Sometimes, a few lessons on historical thinking are incorporated into the course, but it is rare for historical thinking and the development of creativity to be the main objectives of the entire course.

An alternative history classroom that would inspire creativity would look much more like a laboratory or a workshop in which students learn to think like historians by engaging in historical analysis of primary sources. The intent of the course would not be to teach specific information, but to cultivate curiosity and specific skills of interpretation. Historical thinking would take precedence over historical facts. Exams in such a course would not ask students to recall information, but would instead ask them to use the skills they gained in class to interpret historical sources or puzzles not previously encountered. Students would be graded on their ability to provide plausible explanations for complex historical moments.

8   Rethinking History Education
With Photographs and Material
Culture

Sometimes it seems that the only thing students hate more than lectures are discussions, or debates, or presentations, or group projects, or individual projects, or waking up and going to class. I have had some success, however, in maintaining student interest by doing classroom material culture workshops, in which students don't passively absorb information but become historian-detectives who actively try to solve a puzzle.

At an antique store in Hannibal, Missouri, I once bought a pack of about a hundred photographs for $15. Photographs in the collection date from the 1890s to the 1970s. It wasn't clear to me who the people in the pictures were, or if the photos were all connected in some way. I knew, however, that this would be a great exercise for a class to practice thinking like historian-detectives.

In a classroom photograph workshop, I ask students to break into groups of five or six. Usually this exercise works best with a classroom of thirty or forty students, but it can also work in smaller or larger classes. I give each group a handful of the photographs, and I let them know that they can trade their photographs with other groups after they have extracted as much information as they can from the photographs in their possession. I pose two questions to get the groups started: "Are these photographs related?" and "What is the story that they tell?" In attempting to solve the mystery, most groups begin reasonably enough by sorting out the photographs, looking for common faces or names written on the reverse sides. When the going gets tough, students ask me for the answer. But the thing is, I don't know the answer. There is no singular answer; there is only inference from the evidence, and a variety of partial answers. Standards of learning have created a generation of students who can remember and repeat, but who do not yet have the confidence to express new ideas. This lesson is designed to break them from the old orthodoxy of facts. I tell students that it is important for them to recognize the value of their own interpretation. I say that I am only the chief of this classroom detective agency, and it is the task of each of the student-detectives to find an answer to the mystery.[1]

One group will discover a set of six photographs of a boy from the 1930s. Looking deeper, they might discover that it is not just one boy. It appears to be twins, and then, no, triplets. Three names on the back confirm that it is Donald, Larry, and Gerald. Donald has a pen in the front pocket of his overalls, and the top button of his shirt is buttoned; Gerald has a pencil; and Larry has no visible writing utensil. Historical context clues take time to discover, and might not be immediately obvious. The reverse sides of the photographs indicate that there were once two sets of three photographs, and that the two sets were glued to different kinds of paper. One was glued to the black construction paper of a scrapbook album. The other shows lines from lined writing paper. A slight difference in color and contrast indicates that they were kept in different environments; one set is more faded, perhaps from exposure to light, as if it sat in a picture frame near a window.

With each image in the collection, students can piece together the puzzle. They begin to match last names and faces, even across the decades. A porch that appeared in one photo looks like a porch in another. The same girl appears again and again across various photographs, as does her cat. There are pictures of a family blowing out the candles on a birthday cake. There is a photo of a horse in a pasture, kids getting ready for the first day of school, weddings, and family reunions.

I ask whether anyone can write a story about these photographs. No, there is no story here, one student says. A story, he thinks, must be fiction. It must have a beginning and end, a hero and heroine, a castle and a princess. But this is not correct. History is a collection of stories we write ourselves. To be a historian of Donald, Gerald, and Larry, you have to work from these photographs to write a story. Do not leave out what seems inconsequential.

Although the student might struggle at first, they soon establish a setting for the photographs. It is a Caucasian family, perhaps German-American, judging from the last names, living in Missouri and Kansas, mostly during the first half

Figure 8.1 Photograph of Triplets

Looking deeper into a set of photographs reveals more clues about their origin.

of the twentieth century. We chart the important moments in their lives. The photographs don't show any political events or wars, only events in the history of the family. Gradually the story begins to grow, and we can ask more questions. When do you see power lines come to the home? Do they have a car? What might they do for work? Are they a happy family? In the end, we have built a case like detectives might, and we can tell a story. It is a common story about an American farming family and what they care about. Detective work does not always lead to a smoking gun, and stories do not have to end in heroism or tragedy. Most of history—most of American history, in fact—consists of common people farming the soil and going through their daily experiences, concerned with their family members and the communities around them.

The skills of a detective will not easily be replaced by a search engine. Would Sherlock Holmes have used the Internet to solve crimes? Well, certainly he would have done so, if he had thought it would be helpful. But, I'm not sure access to the Internet would have done Sherlock much good. He was always deducing answers logically from what he had seen firsthand, and that kind of information and that kind of logical thought is not (yet!) available on Google. Our quest for information can be aided by technology, but technology does not easily replace skills of interpretation.

Photographs as Clues

Photographs need to be more than illustrations of past events; they also must serve as the sources through which we develop our understanding of the past. In a creative history classroom, we should learn to read photographs like we read texts. We can ask questions about the photographer. Were they a professional or an amateur? Is the camera on a tripod, positioned so the sun shines from behind the photographer? If we switch our focus to the person in the photograph, we can ask even more questions. Does the person appear comfortable having his or her picture taken? What is the relationship between the subject and the photographer? We can learn to read the shadows, read the architecture, read the streetscapes and countrysides for signs of historical context. How people pose, where they take photographs, and what is included in them all tell us something about the society we are studying. We can also ask questions about the history of the physical photographs. Wear and tear patterns can tell us perhaps if a photograph was carried around in a wallet, if it was glued into a scrapbook, or if it sat in at the window sill and was faded by the sun.

Reading the background information of a photograph brings the context to life, and activates our creative sense. Figure 8.2 is a section of a photo from a parade in Holland, Michigan. How could we determine the age of this photo? Perhaps clothing styles, the particular automobile models, a paved or dirt road, the construction of well-known buildings, could all be clues. In this photograph, the flags are of some help dating the scene. Two of the flags in the foreground of the photo can be seen most clearly. The flags are folded,

Forty-five stars
1896-1908

Forty-six stars
1908-1912

Forty-eight stars
1912-1959

Figure 8.2 Flag Stars

Is it possible to date an image from the number of stars on the flag? Be careful: you might be misled.

so it is not possible to count the number of stars directly, but even so, the configuration of the stars gives us a clue. Some research in reference works informs us that before 1908, the bottom row of stars on the American flag was indented on the left. From 1908–1912, the long and short lines of stars were inverted to make room for a star representing a new state. This means that from 1908–1912, the bottom line of stars was longer than the second-to-last line. In fact, this can be seen most clearly in the photo. But in 1912, the forty-seventh and forty-eighth states joined the Union, and the new 48-star flag had lines of stars at equal lengths. The consequence of all this is that a historian might count the stars to determine that this photo was made between 1908 and 1912. Yet, there is still a possibility that the photo dates to sometime after 1912. Just because the flag of 1908–1912 became obsolete in 1912 does not mean that everyone immediately threw away their old flags and bought new 48-star flags.

The dates on placards held by people marching in the parade indicate various graduate classes of the college. These dates are helpful only in a general sense that we can tell the college graduates of 1870 are now old men and women in the photo. Zooming in to another flag in the distance, however, it appears that more evidence can be found to date the photo by the number of stars in the flag. The flag in the little girl's hands (or is it being held by the left hand of a boy in a dark suit with his right hand behind his back?) is a 48-star, post-1912 flag. Evidence for a post-1912 date is mounting. It seems the Hollanders (citizens of Holland, Michigan) were still flying pre-1912 flags in a latter-day parade! Small pieces of evidence, each needing to be interpreted, combine to form a convincing narrative of the past. Evidence, not proof, is what historians are after. "Proof" is a term falsely imported from geometry and other logical sciences. History, as an empirical discipline, does not seek proof, but probability.[2] With all reasonable confidence, the date of this photograph can be narrowed to a particular range.

Similar techniques might help date written sources. At another antique store I purchased an old notebook that a student used during a class in government. In that undated notebook, the student wrote that the president of the United States makes $75,000 per year. I first thought that this fact would be able to help me narrow down the date of the notebook to a reasonable range. But, reference works explain that presidents from Taft through Truman were paid precisely that salary. The student could have composed that line in his notebook at any time between 1909 and 1949 (or potentially after that, if the student was using an out-of-date source). Elsewhere in the notes, however, the student wrote that there is one representative in Congress for every 212,407 people. This ratio was based on the 1910 census and was fixed in 1913. The ratio lasted until 1923. In another instance, the student wrote that the chief justice of the Supreme Court makes $15,000, which fixes a date between 1911 and 1926. Again, an exact date is elusive, but it is possible to use clues to narrow down a range. Historians don't require exact dates or measurements. Like a scientist rounding off numbers to certain significant digits, a historian in most purposes is happy to know roughly when something occurred, or a range of possible dates.

Finding the Answer in a Photograph

If we approach antique store items with curiosity, each might present us with a new historical puzzle, calling for the application of learned techniques of interpretation, or the development of new interpretive techniques. I bought a pile of aerial photographs at an antique store in Staunton, Virginia. The store owner did not know where the photographs came from, and there was no obvious sign of their provenance. This, I knew, would be another set of sources for my students to investigate. Just how much information can we gather from a photograph or from a stack of similar photographs? Can we tell where this is, when the photograph was taken, even perhaps the culture of the place photographed?

Start with the obvious. This appears to be a photo of a middle-class farmstead, with barns, a dirt road, and pine trees. There is no snow, so it is probably not winter, unless this is perhaps an image from somewhere in the South. Can we tell from the architecture if it is an American house? What can we use to

Figure 8.3 Aerial Photograph of Homestead

An aerial photograph of a farmstead, circa 1975. Historians learn to "read" photographs for clues about a time and place.

date the photograph? One possible source for a date is the satellite dish on the property. Satellite dishes were not popular until after 1976. Is there a satellite dish in the image? State license plates used to be uniform in color, so maybe, if we can zoom in on the photo with a magnifying glass, we can identify the state from the license plate. Sometimes we can be thrown off by false clues. Black and white photography is a red herring. Some of us may think that color photography replaced black and white photography suddenly, completely, and permanently. But of course, black and white photography continues still. Sometimes, a historic house might have a construction date, but there is a chance that the information can be false. Historic preservationists know that problem all too well: over time, the original construction date on a house is often lost, so appraisers assign artificial dates, and with some statistical heaping, it appears that a disproportionate share of houses were built in precisely the year 1900. A clever student used an Internet search to identify a series of codes on the reverse of the photograph. The codes led him to a photograph company. He called the company and they confirmed that the series of photographs was taken near Traverse City, Michigan, during the 1970s. As computer technology becomes stronger, it becomes more difficult to teach traditional methods. When you solve a historical problem on your own, you never forget it. Internet research might tell you the same thing, but lessons learned passively rarely stick.

With experience, reading photographs becomes easier and you see things those without experience gloss over. In assembling images for this book, I lost an old photograph that illustrated this well. The photograph was of a woman standing against a white picket fence, and the shadow of the photographer was also visible in the image because the sun was behind the photographer when the photo was taken. The shadow indicated that the photographer had their head down, their elbows tucked: a clear sign that they were looking down into a camera designed like the popular early-twentieth century "brownie." Without the knowledge of how an old camera worked, the shadow would not reveal its secrets. Cameras were once held at chest level, and then, in the later twentieth century, we held the viewfinder at eye level. Now, with smartphones, we take photographs with one hand extended in front of us. Our relationship to photography is ever-changing. Enter an apartment today of a person under 30 years old, and you will find no photographs on display. In time, as digital photography completely replaces film photography, we all lose the sense of the aging of physical artifacts, and we will no longer leave photographs around for future generations to discover and analyze.

Additional Examples of Material Culture Workshops

Teachers might consider replacing traditional discussions of reading with material culture workshops. Relevant objects for historical thinking exercises can easily be found at local antique stores. In addition to photographs, a class might investigate bricks and nails and other building materials, financial papers, a collection of letters, or a box of old toys. The key to such lessons is that they cannot be merely a "show and tell," but must include a sufficient number of related items such that students can draw connections to solve a historical question. Antique stores provide sources for all of these kinds of classroom historical exercises. They are an underutilized resource for learning about history.[3] Here are a few other examples that I have used in my classes:

1. In a small class, or in break-out groups, students are presented with a collection of photographs representing the history of photography. If possible, these artifacts should include actual daguerreotypes or other early images, tintypes, albumens, Kodak prints, negatives on glass, Polaroids, and so on. The images do not need to come from a single place, or relate to each other in any particular way. Students are then asked to place the photographs in chronological order. They learn to recognize clothing, technology, image-type, wear and tear on the photograph, and other signs of a photograph's age such as the style, theme, or subject of the image. A classroom discussion follows, in which we talk about technological change as a major theme of history.
2. Student groups can also analyze a box of old financial documents to help them understand financial, economic, and cultural history. I own a

collection of financial papers dating from the period 1930–1960 from a man who lived on the South Carolina-Georgia border. When I pass out these documents, I ask students to build the life story of this man. I say, "Tell me if he is rich or poor, happy or depressed. Tell me what kind of life he lived, and what he did for a living." Groups compete to build the most likely short biography. Through this exercise, students learn about old checking systems, clearinghouses, war bonds and how they work, inflation, double-entry bookkeeping, and a host of other common financial practices from the mid-century. They discover the paper world that existed before the digital world came into being.

3. Old samples of paper can be used in another exercise in chronology and technology. Students sort old cotton rags and hemp paper from wood-pulp paper. They use dates printed on the materials, signs of wear and tear, and other markings to determine the age of particular pieces of paper. Most of the papers come from old, damaged, tossed-aside books that book dealers can no longer sell, despite or perhaps because of the age of the materials. Such paper is easy to come by if you ask at antique stores and booksellers. In this exercise, students learn about the impact of the market revolution on paper production. They recognize that newspaper print was tiny because it saved paper. They also learn an important lesson about avoiding both presentism (applying present-day values and perspective to judgments of the past) and the progressive view that things have always gotten better. This lesson is that old papers, dating from before the market revolution, were often of much higher quality. But with increased demand for paper in the nineteenth century, cheaper paper needed to be produced, so new types were developed.

4. Students are given copies of an old letter with the signature of a famous historical figure, or a collection of old items ostensibly from this historical figure. They are then tasked with determining if the provenance is real. For determining the legitimacy of a letter, they might investigate handwriting, signatures, ink, paper texture (to determine age), or historical context clues in the text (such as anachronistic words).

5. Take fifteen to twenty physical historical objects, anything from an old vacuum tube to a square nail, a shoehorn, a wooden peg, an ink pot, etc. Try to use items that were once common but are now nowhere in use. Number sheets of paper accordingly and set one object on each sheet of paper. Have the class each try to fill in their own paper with a name and explanation of use for each object. Bring the class together and tally up a winner. Discuss how people used their previous knowledge or sleuthing to identify the items.

Moving away from history as a discipline of memorization, I see it as a discipline of solving problems. Sources provide problems of interpretation, and historians must try to make sense out of sources. Having prepared students to read a variety of materials, visual, and textual sources, teachers should test their ability to discover meaning in similar but new sources. Teachers who wish to inspire historical creativity can ask students to interpret a photograph or another physical object. Is it possible to write a page, an article, or perhaps even a book just on one photograph? I think it is. When teachers present fresh problems on a math exam or ask students to read a passage they've never seen before and provide analysis, it is not considered at all out of the ordinary. Why, then, must history exams ask students to remember data rather than ask them to apply skills to interpret sources they've never seen before? History, like mathematics, is an applied discipline.

Notes

1. A similar example can be heard in the Radiolab Podcast, Season 2, Episode 1: "Detective Stories." www.radiolab.org/2007/sep/10, accessed March 21, 2018. Listen to the segment between minutes 19:00 and 41:00 minutes. An episode of *This American Life* also takes a similar detective-story approach to family history: www.thisamericanlife.org/radio-archives/episode/199/house-on-loon-lake, accessed March 22, 2018.
2. Those who talk about "proof" in history are probably more likely to also use terms like "debunk" when addressing opposing points of view. Here, the idea is that only one side is completely correct, while the other side of the debate is completely incorrect. Arguments about history, while potentially logically incompatible, are more likely to conflict in some but not all areas of interpretation, and are possibly complimentary, not exclusive.
3. Michael J. Douma, "Sorting the Past: The Social Function of Antique Stores as Centers for the Production of Local History" *International Journal of Regional and Local History* 10:2 (2015), 101–119.

9 "Why Men Stopped Wearing Hats" and Other Important Historical Questions

In my mind, there are a few major problems in American history that historians must come back to year after year. Number one: were the founding fathers motivated by their own economic concerns when signing the Constitution? Number two: what was the cause or causes of the American Civil War? Number three: why, in the twentieth century, did American men stop wearing hats? Since the first two questions are perennial topics already receiving significant attention in American history courses, I will pass them over and address the third critical question.

Look at any photograph of a parade or political convention from the 1920s, and you will see men wearing hats. Throughout the nineteenth century and into the first decades of the twentieth, hats were an essential clothing item for most men. Old phrases in our language still attest to the intimate connection between a man's personality and his hat. If I am proven wrong, I "will eat my hat" is one example. There is also the phrase "all hat, no cattle" for someone who appears to be one thing, and acts as another. The days when men all had a personal, recognizable hat to set on the shelf are over. If you look out over a crowd today, you might see a few baseball caps, but it is unlikely that you would see any derbies, fedoras, pork pies, or stove pipe hats. What happened to cause this change? Why did men stop wearing hats?

This question may seem simple and trivial at first. If I bring it up in class, I am always greeted with bewildered looks and half-smiles from students who expect to hear lectures about politics and war.[1] But the history of why men stopped wearing hats is important because it provides an easy to understand, yet unsolved historical query that allows everyone to participate in a debate about historical cause and effect. Because so little has been written on the topic, no one can appeal to a secondary source or to a published argument. It is also quite difficult to find any empirical data to test, so for now it must remain primarily an exercise in theory. "The Hat Problem," I believe, could be the historian's version of Fermat's Last Theorem, a mathematical problem, recently solved, which occupied generations of mathematicians. Of course, there is no "proof" in history as there is in mathematics. Questions about the past can never be solved with perfect confidence. There is only argumentation from the evidence and an ongoing search for more and better evidence.

So, let's work from the evidence and consider a few possible theories for the downfall of the hat. First, there are the social theories. Perhaps men stopped wearing hats because they were out of place in the casual atmosphere of American society in the 1960s and 1970s. This seems like a decent theory, until it becomes apparent that the theory has no real explanatory power. A good historical theory needs to explain cause and effect. To say that men stopped wearing hats because their attitudes changed does not explain why their attitudes changed. A second social theory would have it that the breakdown of social hierarchy encouraged men to avoid such status symbols as hats, since hats (think of the top hat, the farmer's hat, the bourgeois derby) served to reinforce social distinction and inequality. This may be a step in the right direction, but it doesn't explain why men stopped wearing hats in general; it only attempts to explain why men stopped wearing hats that denoted social status. Good theories must be general, like the General Theory of Relativity. Bad theories are not always wrong—they just don't explain everything. Newton's theories, for example, are just as useful as Einstein's for most calculations, but they are incomplete.

Perhaps men stopped wearing hats because of a trend started by American soldiers returning from the Second World War. Perhaps these soldiers refused to wear hats as citizens, because they had tired of wearing uncomfortable hats as soldiers. Now, anecdotal evidence from soldiers may demonstrate that this was the case for a few particular individuals. But it does not stand to reason that all or a majority of returning soldiers would feel the same way and thus initiate a cultural revolution. This final social theory also leaves out the millions of American men who never joined the service, and who would probably not cease their hat-wearing activities in response to the discomfort of these anti-hat ex-soldiers.

Another set of theories explains the disappearance of hats by appealing to changes in the physical environment. A strong contender of this type is the transportation-hat thesis, which argues that in the mid-twentieth century, men began spending much more time indoors, where hats were not needed for protection from weather, and where, in fact, social proscription already curbed the wearing of hats. As a corollary to this idea, men also spent more time in automobiles, in which roofs again freed them from the necessity of covering their heads. Additionally, automobile roofs are low enough to make it nearly impossible to wear high hats anyways. This argument was proffered by National Public Radio's Robert Krulwich.[2]

As the population of cities grew and men spent more time in urban landscapes, they found themselves constantly removing their hats, which were a burden to carry. Despite its attractiveness, this thesis does have its flaws, however. Much of the growth of population in urban centers was already occurring earlier in the century. People had worked indoors in factories for generations, and people already traveled in covered carriages in the nineteenth century. Yet, these urban commuters still wore hats. In fact, it could be argued that by 1900, hats were worn not for protection from weather but as fashion statements—marks of social class and position.

The sunglasses thesis is of a similar type. Modern sunglasses were invented in 1929 and become popular in the 1930s. It is perhaps possible that in decades to follow, sunglasses replaced hats as the preferred technology for keeping sun out of our eyes. The push to sell sunglasses in Atlantic City to tourists and rich folks in the 1930s, the 1959 trademark, and the 1960s ad campaigns were integral to the rise of the hat's rival: Ray-Bans!

But maybe instead of environmental and social factors, we need to summon economics to explain the decline of the hat wearers. An economic thesis might propose that the increasing division of labor and the growing extent of the market led to the decline of hat-wearing professions. In the nineteenth century, not only bakers, brewers, and butchers wore hats, but so did tradesmen of all varieties. As white-collar jobs appeared in the modern industrial economy, fewer workers needed to signal their trade and their social standing with a specific kind of hat. Many jobs that previously required hats went out of existence.

Then again, there is the hygiene thesis, which has a socio-economic rationale as well. Hats, it could be argued, were used to keep men clean. They kept the dust and rain off men's hair. This was in a day when indoor plumbing was uncommon, and most folks bathed infrequently. In the modern age, people began to shower daily and could afford cheap shampoo, so they didn't worry as much about getting dirty, so long as they could clean themselves.

There are also potential cultural theories to consider. One could argue that mass media portrayals of famous, good-looking hatless men like James Dean and John F. Kennedy set the tone for a new modern hatless male. On television and in film, hats would only obscure the face of the presenters, actors, and politicians, so hats were removed for the sake of presentation and rating. This is a top-down (pun intended) explanation, and it requires you to believe that men were quite susceptible to trends. There is some power in explanations from fashion, explanations that might explain similar phenomenon today, like the question about why more American men are bearded now than ten years ago, and when and why we hit "peak beard." Trends, as well, can only be identified once they appear, so by explaining the decline of hat-wearing by suggesting that it was a trend, is really to say nothing all that clear about cause and effect.

If we are to accept that theory, we should also consider the hair theory, which states that men removed their hats because they wanted to show their hair. This argument, however, probably confuses cause and effect, or is a classic chicken-and-the-egg situation. Which came first: men who wanted to wear a pompadour and therefore chose to stop wearing a hat, or men who stopped wearing hats and therefore chose to style their hair as a pompadour? (No one should ever accuse me of avoiding the hard questions!) An additional cultural thesis has its own logical errors. Some say that the hat symbolized an older generation, the "milliner generation," and this is why hats were no longer worn. Well, then, I must ask, why did the generation of 1890 not see the hat-wearing phenomenon of the generation of 1860 as old-fashioned, and respond by casting off their hats? What made mid-twentieth century men react differently?

On their own, none of these theories seems completely satisfactory and exhaustive, but perhaps some combination of the theories is sufficiently convincing. Now, the problem is how to decide which theories to include. If we are to list, say, the top three or the top five reasons why men stopped wearing hats, the new combined theory would still be incomplete. It would not take into consideration that some guy in Alaska stopped wearing hats in a bet to see if he could make it through a winter bare-headed. The new theory would have to consider whether a change in the average size of the American male head had an effect on the total number of hat-wearers, since maybe big-headed people felt constricted wearing common hats as hat-makers failed to adjust marketed hat sizes to fit to the new standard cranium. In the end, there may be millions of reasons why men stopped wearing hats. Is it possible to disaggregate the causes? Is it possible to say one cause is more important than another? This is a real methodological problem for historians. The best theses are usually complex enough to balance many factors of change, and yet simple enough to be readily understood. It doesn't help, for example, if a historian says that there are an infinite number of reasons why change came about, or that a situation is too complex to arrive at any thesis. Some historians make the mistake of presenting no thesis at all, and say instead that the events were "complicated." This is nothing short of admitting defeat. An historian who cannot explain change is no historian at all.

How would a political scientist or a statistical historian answer this question? By appealing to data, of course, with which one could run a regression and find a significant correlation. Unfortunately, data of this kind is difficult to find. Perhaps it can be done, although I leave the search for data to someone else. What they need to do is set some time parameters to determine an estimate of when the change occurred. Then, they need to see if there are regional differences. Did the change take place more or less simultaneously across the country, or did the trend spread from one part of the country to the others? But even with unlimited data, a satisfactory explanation might be elusive.

A student in my college class responded to this challenge with a cynical, but good-hearted and intelligent quip.

> After an extensive review of the literature from the foremost hat authorities, one would deduce that it is unfair to attribute the decline to a single cause.

Later in the essay, he continued:

> The hatless revolution was not welcomed by all, though. Many hat factories shut down as a result of rapid sales decline, resulting in some very mad hatters. The hatters were so mad in fact, that the hat museum of Stockport, in Great Britain, has reported that workers "verbally berated" anyone so unfortunate as to walk through the town of Stockport without a hat.

Amused, I never bothered to check the historical accuracy of this last statement. In my opinion, though, the student was more or less correct that there is no single cause of men no longer wearing hats. The task of the historian is to render the complexities of the past into an understandable narrative or analysis. To do so, historians use empirical data to support theory.

Without sufficiently convincing data, we need to posit hypothetical explanations and consider the logic of the proposed cause and effect mechanism. In this way, we work deductively to consider the possibility of hypothesis.

To be creative as historians, we sometimes need to ask seemingly silly questions like "Why did men stop wearing hats?" We must be willing to have fun and to play around with new topics. Creativity and humor open new avenues for the production of knowledge. The biggest problem for young historians is that they often think there is only one story to tell, and that it has to be simple. But once they realize that history is complex, arguable, contested, and incomplete, there is a lot of room for perspective. There are many unsolved historical problems that require the production of new history, and it does no harm to take them up with a bit of humor. Some of my favorite articles are satirical, but they also prove real points. For example, the article "Common-Law Origin of the Infield Fly Rule," satirizes legal writing with its overuse of footnotes and asides into seemingly irrelevant topics. An article titled "The Influence of Immanuel Kant on Evidentiary Approaches in Eighteenth Century Bulgaria" is a half-serious response to a politician's quip about the absurdity of minor topics in the history of philosophy.[3] "A Few Goodmen: Surname-Sharing Economist Coauthors" might be the authors' most-read work.[4]

A historian seeks to find the most likely explanation, the dominant cause of change. There are times, however, when historical solutions are not so easy to find, and there are questions which cannot be clearly answered. The "Hat Problem" or the "Hat Question" may remain forever unanswered.

Historical Questions to Ponder

The good thing about questions of this type is that no one enters the conversation from a privileged position of knowing the answer, and neither the answer nor good empirical data on the topic is readily available online. Lectures on such historical problems can be followed by debate or discussion periods. A class can be a participatory workshop, where each person can contribute to shaping the collective meaning of a historical episode. When topics are fun and essentially democratic (since no one, even the professor, probably has a perfectly correct answer), the attempt to solve the problem is not bound up with any prescribed textbook answer or view of an authority.

Here is another question a class might ponder. Why do older scholars list things on a CV in descending order (oldest first, newest at the bottom of a list), while younger scholars tend to create lists in ascending order—that is, with the most recent date at the top of a list? At some point in time, the common practice changed, but why did this happen? What caused this change?[5]

One common answer to this question is that the changeover from typewriters to computers effected this change. The reasoning seems to be that when people wrote a CV on a typewriter, they would leave room at the bottom of a list, and it was easier to add extra lines about new publications or new jobs to the list later on. To me, this is quite unconvincing. I have seen many older CVs included in archival collections, and I don't recall ever seeing a typed example with extra space available at the bottom of a list. Nor does this "typewriter" explanation seem to make sense from a practical time-saving perspective. Why would a prepared list in ascending or descending order be easier to add material to?

Searches online don't seem to offer any good explanations for this change. A lot of people explain that it is better to list items in reverse chronological order. Considering the lessons in chapters one and two of this book, we may note how curious it is that a person would think of ascending or descending order as chronological and its opposite as reverse chronological. Which one is which? These are the kinds of vague or ambiguous terms that frustrate young children on classroom exams. It can be very frustrating for those who don't see the world the same way as the person writing the instructions.

Apparently, a lot of people think it doesn't matter whether a job applicant lists items in ascending or descending order, but these people are clearly wrong, since there are indeed other people who *do* think that it matters a lot. And if some people think it matters, then it must matter, because there is a good chance that when others read your CV, some of them are going to be people who are genuinely concerned about these things. For example, in response to a question about the proper order for listing academic achievements, Karen Kelsky, of the website "The Professor is In," writes:

> [Y]ou must not, under any circumstances, ever change the principle of reverse chronological order. That one act alone could definitively damage your standing and credibility. The point here, if it's not clear, is that you should always be gunning for "the next big thing" so that you have highly prestigious grants/awarded within the top 3 or so grants on a cyclical or ongoing basis. This is why academics have ulcers.[6]

The shift in ordering material on a CV might reflect the advice of some popular published guide to academic writing or résumé writing which declared a preference for one style of chronological ordering over another, thereby shaping a generation of writers. In addition, with the speed of technological change ever increasing, older items on the CV became less relevant than they had been in years before. A résumé from 1980, for example, is more likely to be able to list relevant skills and jobs from the 1950s than is a résumé from 2010 likely to list relevant skills and jobs from the 1980s.

I have a tentative and somewhat incomplete alternative explanation for the switchover from descending to ascending order in academic CVs. Up until, say, the 1990s, academic search committees received only a few job applications for each search and they could manageably read them all, taking time to see the progression in a candidate's career. Then, however, the supply of scholars grew, far outstripping demand, so that search committees faced a daunting task of reading one hundred or more CVs for each job opening. Scholars who put their new publications visibly at the top of the page had a better chance of getting seen. So, academics responded to the growing impatience and cursory examination of the records by reversing the order of their presentation.

Other uncommon topics that might lead to similar serious historical discussions are the following.

1. Which came first: the automobile or the gas station? And which came first: "the can opener or the can?" These may seem like chicken-or-the-egg questions, but they can stimulate some interesting discussion and possible answers.
2. How did the medieval Norse die out in Greenland? (This requires some background on the possibilities: plague, Inuit attack, starvation, climate change, pirate attacks, migration to North America, migration to Iceland, etc.). This may be better debated after introducing some background readings.
3. What was the origin of the American log cabin? (Again, this takes some background reading or lecture presentation. The competition of influences is among Swiss, German, English, Czech, French, and Scandinavian styles. A related question is: "How likely is it that the same architectural style or technology will develop separately in multiple locations?"

I like questions that can be answered many ways, and which have not been the focus of too much historical attention. I like historical questions that students can ponder and prod with logic and thought experiments. Questions about the everyday effects of history on cultural life are the best in this regard. So, consider that Americans in their commute to work always seem to be driving into the sun. Although I know of no data on this topic, it seems that more Americans live to the west of where they work than to the east. Suburbs, for example, tend to be larger on the west side of a city. As a result, we drive into the sun in the morning on the way to work, and into the sun again in our afternoon or evening commutes home. Partly, this can be explained by the east-west orientation of the United States. Our cities are more likely to be stretched along an east-west axis, than a north-south axis, simply because the main current of movement in the country's history has been to the west, to new lands. Cities on the East Coast could not have suburbs develop to the east because the Atlantic Ocean gets in the way. This means that on the East Coast, it is certainly more true than anywhere else that people drive into the sun twice a day. Do American cities in the Midwest, the South, and the Great Plains follow similar patterns, in which suburban growth is greater to the west than in any other direction? Is there a way to solve this question? Can we know for sure if this is indeed the case, or have I only imagined it? Perhaps a student knows of a method that I am not aware of.

Good questions lead to open debates. While debates about these kinds of questions are unlikely to lead to answers, they promote debate skills and historical thinking. If people are motivated to win an argument, they will do research on their own and come to their own positions. Weeks of arguments about historical interpretation will turn students into historians in a faster, better way than will weeks of presented historical content alone. If a class is presented with a tailor-made historical question that they might be able to answer, students are likely to voluntarily spend time outside of class coming up with solutions.

Notes

1. There has been precious little written on the history of the hat, and there is not likely soon to be an endowed chair of Hat History at Harvard, although the first choice for such a position should be the University of Al Quaraouiyine in Fez, Morrocco. The historiography does contain a few choice lines, however, such as this one from Michael Harrison's *The History of the Hat* (London: Herbert Jenkins, 1960), 14: "Man long ago devised a method of taking needed shade with him—and invented the hat." The birth of the hat is certainly an event of ancient times, and is long obscured by the ages, but the death of the formal hat is quite recent.
2. Robert Krulwich, "Who Killed Men's Hats? Think of a Three Letter Word Beginning with 'I'" www.npr.org/sections/krulwich/2012/05/04/152011840/who-killed-mens-hats-think-of-a-three-letter-word-beginning-with-i (originally posted May 4, 2012, accessed on November 8, 2015).
3. "Common-Law Origins of the Infield Fly Rule," *University of Pennsylvania Law Review* 123 (1975), 1474–1481; Orin S. Kerr, "The Influence of Immanuel Kant on Evidentiary Approaches in Eighteenth Century Bulgaria," 2015. http://ssrn.com/abstract=2586464, accessed March 21, 2018.
4. See also Allen C. Goodman, Joshua Goodman, Lucas Goodman, and Serana Goodman, "A Few Goodmen: Surname-Sharing Economist Coauthors." http://scholar.harvard.edu/files/joshuagoodman/files/goodmans.pdf, accessed on November 26, 2015. H.L. Mencken's bathtub hoax spread far and wide a supposedly correct history of the bathtub. A famous nonsensical paper by Alan Sokal, titled "Transgressing the Boundaries: Towards a Transformative Hermeneutics of Quantum Gravity," was submitted to the journal *Social Text* to prove that its peer-review process was faulty. Likewise, satirical journals like *The Journal of Irreproducible Results* and *The Journal of Universal Rejection* ridicule academia and prove a point about what good scholarship and practice should be.
5. A related problem is our language of what we mean by ascending or descending, and what we mean when we speak of moving an event back or forward, back meaning further in the future, and forward, meaning closer to the present. At least, that's how I see it, but others might disagree. Especially across cultures, saying that you want to "move a meeting back to Tuesday" might be pretty confusing. For example, speakers of Aymara, a native language of South America, conceive of the future being behind and the past being ahead. Rafael E. Nunez and Eve Sweetser, "With the Future Behind Them: Convergent Evidence from Aymara Language and Gesture in the Crosslinguistic Comparison of Spatial Construals of Time" *Cognitive Science* 20 (2006), 401–450.
6. Karen Kelsky, "Dr. Karen's Rules of the Academic CV," January 15, 2012. http://theprofessorisin.com/2016/08/19/dr-karens-rules-of-the-academic-cv/, accessed March 20, 2017.

10 Classroom History Diagrams

Give data to students & ask them to communicate it visually.

On the eve of the Civil War, most Americans held ambivalent views about the nature of slavery and its persistence in the nation. Some Americans were slaveholders or abolitionists, but most Southerners did not own slaves, and most Northerners did not identify with the abolitionist cause. For years, I made this point in my lectures, and yet, when I read my students' exams, they continued to make the mistake of thinking all Americans had once been either slaveholders or abolitionists. Then one semester, when I introduced the diagram of Figure 10.1, this confusion seemed to disappear.

When a question about slavery came up on the final exam, nearly half of the class referred to this diagram or even drew it.

I am convinced of the great power of visualizations in creative historical thinking. Graphic designer Edward Tufte argues that graphics are more than "devices for showing the obvious to the ignorant," but are actually "instruments for reasoning about information."[1] In other words, graphics do more than show data; they also reveal it.

A good graphic takes advantage of our ability to reason metaphorically and grounds abstract concepts in basic experience. Graphics metaphorically represent quantities in terms of heights, thicknesses of lines, or sizes of bubbles. Graphics can represent historical information more densely and more clearly than does text. For example, a print table or a text might be difficult to read, or require a thousand words to express clearly all the information that can be demonstrated in a good chart.

Representations of historical data in graphic form are often so natural that we hardly recognize the mental processes at work. The diagram of views of slavery shown in Figure 10.1 lacks a title, and the x- and y- axes are not labeled. Yet many automatically recognize that the height of the curve symbolizes number of persons. The diagram tells us that there were more people who defended slavery than just the slaveholders, and that while many opposed slavery to some extent, they did not necessarily call for its abolition. The diagram also has its limitations. It doesn't tell us, for example, how well-developed these views were, the regional distribution of pro- and anti-slavery sentiments, or the variations within these traditions. All models are necessarily imperfect representations of reality. Diagrams carry essential meaning, but

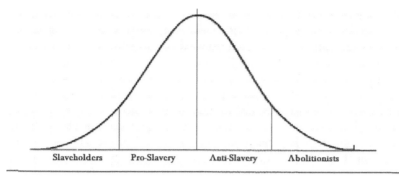

| Slaveholders | Pro-Slavery | Anti-Slavery | Abolitionists |

Figure 10.1 Slavery Bell Curve

The bell curve of antebellum anti-slavery.

as symbolic representations, they always carry limited information selected from a larger set of data. They reinforce learning, they make the stories easier to follow, and they help us retain information. Images are not a crutch for the imagination; they motivate it.[2]

Simple diagrams are easily understood and become the dominant metaphors for cultural understanding. Consider a typical left-right political diagram. It is a straight line that represents views along a spectrum from left to right, from communism to socialism to capitalism and finally fascism. This is, of course, a much too simplistic view of politics. The diagram does not adequately represent all of the nuances or possible political positions. Many recognize these limits, but for many purposes the basic left-right diagram has remained a useful and dominant metaphor in political thought. Those on the left use it to link capitalists with fascists, while those on the right use it to identify socialists with communism. How easily our mental concepts can be overturned, however, with a new diagram. When Hannah Arendt viewed communism and fascism, she saw that they were not on the opposite ends of some political spectrum, but had much in common. She labeled these extremes totalitarian. With a few simple marks on the board, a professor can bend the left and right ends of the spectrum upwards, connecting them. A new category emerges, and the far left and right now appear more similar than disconnected.

Diagrams in history class are better when they are quick and easy to draw. Unlike published infographics, they don't need labels and clutter, so long as the professor properly explains the bounds and metrics of the diagram. Diagrams that are too simple, like Venn diagrams or simply a list divided into two columns of information, run the risk of not being memorable. Creative diagrams that take advantage of simple shapes but add new elements to a traditional view are best. In the design industry, printed diagrams that require explanation are poor diagrams. But in a classroom, diagrams don't need to stand alone. In fact, diagrams that require a bit of explanation require sharp attention from the audience. Diagrams in the class can be put to use or tested. They can be filled-in or altered according to the situation. The key with classroom diagrams is that students should wrestle with them mentally, so that they can see the diagram's application. The diagram is a window into a discussion.

The Matrix

Of all the possible diagrams used in the classroom, perhaps the matrix is the most simple and easy to use. I know an economics professor who claims that he can teach all introductory microeconomics using 2×2 matrices (Figure 10.2). I don't doubt him. Matrices are useful ways of presenting information. They help us see a variety of relationships, and make it easier to remember and compare positions. Clear thought begins with good distinctions, and matrices are about overlapping distinctions onto one another. So a matrix—either 1×2, 2×2, 4×4, or whatever—comes naturally when there are two or more aspects or variations to consider. Matrices help with analytical clarity. They help us explore distinctions and variations; they help us see new ways when we have to fill in the empty squares—exploring the logical space, as it were. Thinking in terms of matrices or conceptual space can help you to realize that there's something "missing" in how we talk or think about things.

A larger table or matrix can be useful to structure an entire lecture, or to prepare for an exam. For instance, I like to use a 4×4 matrix (Figure 10.3) to compare the anti-slavery views of William Lloyd Garrison, Hinton Helper, Stephen Douglas, and Lysander Spooner. These four men had competing views of why American slavery was wrong, how the slavery crisis in the United States could be solved, and how soon it would be preferable to make significant political changes concerning slavery. By structuring these four positions in a table, it is easier to recall more information. In addition, the diagram helps us make comparisons and recognize possibilities. Tables larger than this may present too much information, and can be overwhelming.

Figure 10.2 2×2 Matrix

A 2×2 matrix inspires attempts to fill in missing squares, to see comparison, to fill in the logic possibilities of a problem. What is "valuable and new"?

	Garrison	Helper	Stephen Douglas	Spooner
Grounds for Opposition to Slavery	Moral, Natural Rights	Economic	Politically Impractical	Constitutional, Natural Rights
Method for Ending Slavery	Political, Social Changes	Recolonization	Popular Sovereignty	Compensation or Violence
Time Preference	Immediate	Medium	Long-term	Immediate

Figure 10.3 4×4 Matrix

A 4×4 matrix helps to organize data. This diagram shows the views of four anti-slavery proponents with differing motivations and ideas about how to end slavery.

Typology Diagrams

Diagrams can help us sift and sort information and find meaningful patterns when we are not sure if patterns are there to be found. I learned this firsthand during the fall and winter of 2013, when I developed an interest in interpreting the meaning of historic inscriptions at Virginia's Grand Caverns, the oldest tourist cave in the United States. The names of thousands of visitors are scribbled and inscribed on the walls of the caverns. Some names, dating as early as 1808, are engraved in the form of typeset letters, the red walls carefully scarred to reveal a white rock underneath. Some names were hastily scribbled in pencil, or cut quickly into the surface by the edge of a knife, forming large loopy letters that indicate little concern for penmanship. There are last names without first names, and first names without last names, as well as names of towns and cities from across Virginia and the Mid-Atlantic region. The collection of inscriptions seemed to present a decent balance of two hundred years of voices from the American East Coast. It looked like a record of the area and the country.

Like a child at play, I began to piece together the giant puzzle of the cave's writings. Instead of just collecting all the names in the cave, as others had attempted to do, I thought I might be able to discover structural patterns that explain them. We have enough lists; what we need is meaning, I thought. After sorting the inscriptions into categories I discovered that the shape of inscribed letters, their messages, content, and clarity predictably varied across time. After empirical work of photographing and comparing inscriptions, I developed a typology expressed in Figure 10.4, which gives visual representation to the structure that I believe I discovered in the inscriptions in Grand Caverns.

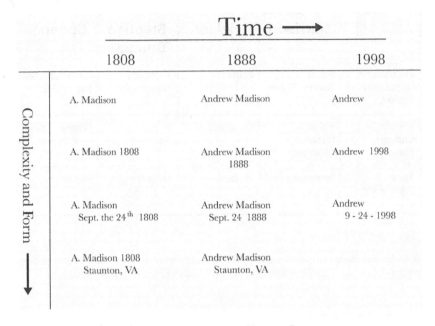

Figure 10.4 Typology of Historic Inscriptions in Virginia Cave

A typology of historic inscriptions on a cave in Virginia.

The typology of historic inscriptions in the Grand Caverns shows in general form how patterns of carving names changed over time. In the beginning of the nineteenth century, many identified foremost by their last name, and so the first name was often given as only an initial. In this typology diagram, Andrew Madison serves as a hypothetical inscriber. In 1808, if he had time to carve more than just his own name, he would likely add a date with the month spelled out. He was also likely to leave a place name. Later in the century, however, most inscribers began writing out their full names. By the late twentieth century, inscriptions became seen as graffiti, and so inscribers hid their last names. The form of giving the date had also changed, and the inscriber seldom listed his hometown. Digging into this typology, we can propose various reasons for why these changes occurred. The diagram contains data, but it inspires explanation to fill in the cause and effect that links the data.

Trees, Fans, and Doodles

History diagrams often include a representation of the element of time. They can draw on metaphors like a web, a tree, a river, or a pile of brick. We are all familiar with a "family tree." But why do we choose this metaphor, with all of its roots and branches? Why does time in the family tree generally flow down, from the branches to the root, when timelines in western society moved instead from left to right? As we work backwards in generations to fill in our family tree, the branches multiply so that it quickly becomes too complicated and impractical to trace more than four or five generations back. The branches of family trees disappear in our mental images. If we can trace one lineage back for centuries, our available data is typically only names, dates of birth, location of birth or marriage, and the like. What we know about the people is limited.

I like to imagine a different kind of family tree. Like a Mandelbrot set, the tree's branches rapidly divide into twigs, and the twigs divide again and again until they disappear. A family tree's branches or roots disappear in the recesses of time, not necessarily with the last recorded names, but with the oldest myths and stories of our families, or with the oldest photographic records. Many Americans have family trees that are sharply disrupted by the moment of migration, when the family was uprooted and transplanted in the New World.

Genealogical diagrams, commonly with a tree metaphor, can help us see history in a new light. Genealogy is almost never taught in an academic setting, and is unfairly considered the realm of amateurs. Most people are familiar with tree diagrams or tournament-style diagrams that show genealogical descent. Family tree diagrams can be beneficial in showing how quickly an ancestor database might expand. The diagram leads to discussions about whether ancestor expansion is truly exponential. A genealogical map places the individual at the center and quickly shows relationships to a wide array of ancestors.[3]

A final kind of neglected graphic is the doodle. I think doodling is not so much a sign of boredom, but a mental call for structure. As data goes whizzing by, we grab some and put it down in diagram form. My student notes from Civil War lectures are full of battleground maps that quickly tell of the nature of the battle. Doodling may consist of lines, images, numbers, or even just a practiced signature. Doodles without clear purpose in their form, like squiggly lines, are the mind's way of priming itself as it searches for something interesting to say. I once undertook a study of nineteenth-century books in the Shenandoah Valley, particularly to look at their inscriptions and marginalia. Doodles in these books consisted of pen-priming marks, where a writer has just dipped the tip of an ink-pen in the ink and is now checking the pen. There were flags, feathers, math problems, poems, architectural drawings, and all kinds of silly faces sketched in the margins. Doodles in these books represented casual artistic creations in moments of idleness. Doodling is a form of creativity that leads to useful diagrams. In classrooms, when students are taking notes, doodling should be generally encouraged.

Notes

1. Edward R. Tufte, *The Visual Display of Quantitative Information*, 2nd edition (Cheshire, CT: Graphics Press, 2002), 53.
2. Tufte, 182.
3. A. Montgomery Johnston, "Genealogy: An Approach to History" *The History Teacher* 11:2 (February 1978), 193–200 (page 196).

Section IV

The Consequences of Creative History

The central theme of this book has been history envisioned as metaphor. To explain historical events and processes, we look for metaphorical links to simpler examples of cause and effect. By way of metaphorical language, historians make connections between the known and the unknown.

This section, beginning with Chapter 11, argues that people mistake the nature of historical change when they attempt to apply one single metaphor to all of History. Those who choose their favorite metaphor for historical change and apply it too rigorously tend towards a myopic view of cause and effect. The simplicity of single metaphors for change is attractive for ideologues, and is often at the root of their dogmatism.

Chapter 12 is concerned with diagrams, which can be used in classrooms to help illustrate principles of history and inspire creative historical thinking.

Chapter 13 argues that to rescue history education from charges of irrelevance, boredom, or elitism, we should explain the discipline by way of analogies of history as music, detective work, and law.

Chapter 14 serves as a conclusion for the book, restating the main argument, and expressing the need for all of us to develop our creativity through play. The recognition that we can discover and create our own argued perspectives should be liberating for all of those who worry that others might take control of their history.

pattern seeking — student response
to data

Does history have a shape? A purpose?

11   Can There Be One Metaphor
for All of History?

A kind of history called "speculative" or "universal" history proposes that History itself has a kind of shape or purpose. Humans are pattern-seeking creatures, but by seeking simple patterns in history, we run the risk of too rigidly applying basic metaphors to explain much deeper complexities of historical change. Speculative history, I argue in this chapter, suffers from "patternicity"—what Michael Shermer defined as "finding meaningful patterns in meaningless noise."[1] The dominant metaphors of speculative history are lines, stages, and cycles. Conceived of as a line, history is said to have a beginning, end, and a direction. Conceived of as stages, history is said to be divisible, subject to deep-seated structural changes. Conceived of as cyclical, history is said to repeat or preserve universal conditions.

Before the modern era, cyclical views of history were quite common. Tied to the seasons and the repetition of nature, the world seemed to mirror the regular, repeating patterns of the cosmos. The illusion of cosmological stability led to the view that history did not seem to progress in any particular direction, towards any particular goal.[2]

Within the Judeo-Christian tradition, however, history is presented as having an overall structure and direction. Augustine of Hippo, in the *City of God*, developed what became the dominant Christian understanding of the shape of history. Augustine conceived of history as a line, with a beginning (a genesis), an end and a direction. In Western Civilization, this became the dominant metaphor of history, with profound implications. Modern progressivism is an heir to this teleological "history as a line, with direction and purpose." While in the Christian view, history moves towards judgment day, in the progressive mind, the world moves inexorably towards some undefined preferred state of being. The progressive view usually admits that historical change comes in fits and starts, and that change does not always mean social progress. But faith in the near inevitability of progress, of constant improvement, while essential to progressivism, is alien to the Christian view of the fall of humanity, and runs counter to the dominant view in much of Western history, in which Europeans looked back and saw their decline from the days of the Roman Empire.

If history develops linearly, and it has a direction, it needs a source of propulsion, a force pushing it in a certain direction. Generally, this force has been sought in conflict. For Augustine in *Civitas Dei*, it was the heavens in conflict with the earth that required a solution. For the German philosopher Hegel, the force moving history forward was the conflict between a state of society and its opposite (a thesis and antithesis) that created a friction that needed to be resolved. As each conflict worked itself out in this Hegelian dialectic, it naturally led to another conflict, ultimately with the goal of working out the spirit of reason and freedom. Hegel's history could therefore be understood as having directionality, an ultimate end, and yet, also some structure. Cyclical history also looks for a force of propulsion. For historians like H.G. Wells and A.J. Toynbee, the force was a similar "challenge and response" mechanism. The trouble with this metaphorical view of history is that it seems that progress can only happen if we agree on some objective standard of value, some absolute value on which to base history. A common progressive view of history popular in the nineteenth century combines directionality (progress upwards or forwards) with fixed stages of development from savagery to barbarism to civilization.

While there are many people today who are essentially historicists who deny ultimate purpose or direction of history, the progressive view remains strong, especially within the historical profession. The leading text of progressive history today may be Jo Guldi and David Armitage's *The History Manifesto*.[3] Guldi and Armitage call on their fellow historians to look at history over the *longue durée*, and to use digital tools to analyze and discover patterns of data and context. Although the book calls for a democratic ethos in the history, it betrays as well an elitist tone, positing learned historians as the true arbiters of cause and effect and as the most qualified guides to policymaking. In a brilliant review of the book, Knox Peden explains that while Guldi and Armitage encourage diversity of subfields and approaches to history, they ultimately believe in a single composite model of history that is both dogmatically progressive and short on humility.[4] The anonymous blogger Pseudoerasmus is less kind. He outlines a host of errors in the book and suggests that Guldi and Armitage's historical method essentially comes down to using "selective anecdotes and impressions which can be cited to bolster some argument that can't be defended conventionally."[5] These criticisms indicate how historians might be blinded by single, grand explanations of history.

Like directionality of history, historical periodization appears subject to the whims of philosophers, numerologists, and gnostics. Historians who believe that history develops in stages look for the laws by which one stage gives way to the next. Prediction and implementations are its true goals—but prediction is the alchemy of history: always a goal, but never within reach. For those who want to regulate and control society, speculative history and the search for laws or patterns has a particular attraction. It promises some special or esoteric knowledge. It promises the power to shape worlds. In the case of the *History Manifesto*, it promises a successful set of progressive policies. Imagining that they "see" a structure in history, social engineers use terms like "history shows" or "history demonstrates." They treat history as one thing, and one thing indivisible without liberty or interpretation for all. The historian Herbert Butterfield, warning about the Whig interpretation of history (the progressive view of history in his day), said that historians can too easily "draw lines through certain events" and that they must be careful not "to forget that this line is merely a mental tick" which doesn't represent causation.[6]

Stages are a common metaphor in the supposed patterns of history. August Comte, the founder of sociology, sought a "social physics" to discover rules governing the succession and coexistence of phenomenon. Comte's unit of study was the group, not the individual. He proposed a three-stage theory with stages labeled as theological, metaphysical, and positive. But other philosophers of history have developed their own stage models, sometimes with three, sometimes with five, sometimes with many more stages of history writ large. But why should we trust, say, Vico or Comte, and not, say, Locke, or Hegel, Marx, Spengler, H.G. Wells, W.W. Rostow, or any of the others who propose conflicting stage theories, and who were all equally confident in their own theories? Locke saw a cyclical pattern in the rise and fall of nations, while Spengler saw civilization rising and falling. For Toynbee, it was also civilizations that developed in thousand-year patterns. Why exactly it had to be one thousand years is unclear. I suspect it is because we are pattern-seeking creatures and one thousand sounds better than 986. All too often, perceived historical patterns correspond with round numerical units like ten, twenty, sixty, or one hundred. Soviet economist Nikolai Kondratiev, for example, proposed observable economic patterns of 40–60 years, a rather flexible length of time.[7] There is also the question of scale: will patterns of history emerge by studying nations, civilizations, or cultures, and how will we define the boundaries of these concepts? These are all problems that speculative history struggles to find a solution for.

Speculative theories present an ultimate heuristic or guide for history, but they can hardly be justified empirically. Because the start and end points of historical stages are vague or imprecise, they often hardly have any predictive capability (Figure 11.1). They are imaginary structures imposed by the viewer. These theories often treat civilizations as units, as historical facts, and they demarcate specific times for events, rather than recognizing that history is made of processes as much as particular events. They then seek patterns and numerological significance. They aim for understanding aggregate action, if not completely determined action, to explain all historical change.

There is nothing natural or inevitable about certain patterns. Mostly, the patterns and chronologies we propose are ones that fit our own preference. History textbooks, for example, tend to break American history into two arbitrary periods, from the colonial era to 1865 (or sometimes 1877), and from that point to the modern day. This makes it easier to teach American history as a series of two courses. But what if we decide to break American history into three periods (colonial, early republic to World War I, and World War I to the present)? American history is sometimes divided into the administrations of forty-five presidents. But we get a different perspective to the same story if we break this history into tenures of seventeen Supreme Court chief justices,

Stage Theories of History

Vico	Gods	Heroes	Man	
Hegel	Oriental	Classical	Germanic	
Comte	Theological	Metaphysical	Positive	
Marx	Classical	Feudal	Capitalist	Socialist
Scottish	Gatherers	Pastoralism	Agriculture	Commerce
Progressive	Savagery	Barbarism	Civilized	Enlightened

Figure 11.1 Stage Theories of History

Stage theories of history propose large general blocks of historical time, distinguished from other periods.

or 116 U.S. Congresses, which might be more insightful. We could also break this history into thematic periods like the Gilded Age and Progressive Era. For national history, we might suggest one form of periodization, for evolutionary history another, for autobiography a third. Periodization happens after the fact, and is neither natural nor inevitable.

Akin to the teleological history and stage theories is the view that people can be on the "right" or "wrong" side of history. What this means exactly is a bit unclear, as the phrase "the wrong side of history" is often meant to suggest that a person holds on to an old immoral view that is bound to give way to a new moral view.[8] After the election of Donald Trump, Barack Obama said that history is not always a straight line, that sometimes it goes backwards or sideways. Obama's warnings about the threats to the nation were poignant, but this language presupposes an ultimate direction or framework for the development of history that might not in fact exist. If history is going sideways or backwards, it begs the question: what it is moving relative to? History itself does not create morality nor determine it, and just because we appear to be moving towards the acceptance of one or another ethical view does not mean that that view is correct. Theories of progress in history are shaped by ethical premises of the present, as we judge other ages by our own standards.[9]

Unfortunately, it seems that the way to get recognized as a great historian is to propose some grand pattern that structures all of history according to mechanical, deterministic designs. Historians who minutely detail the nuances of historical events are less likely to gain popularity because they don't give us the satisfaction of having provided an easy answer. But Frederick

Jackson Turner with his broad "Frontier Thesis," Alexander Gerschenkron with his "Economic Backwardness," Thomas Piketty with his deceptively simple formula r > g, all propose some great single force responsible for moving history. Perhaps these are easier to remember than the works of say an Edward Gibbon or Henri Pirenne, in which a multitude of forces bear on the shape of history. It seems that despite it all, we prefer simplicity in our explanations. The historian Herbert J. Muller wrote: "Analysts are always prone to reduce the many forces to the action of a single force, such as race, environment, or economic activity, and then to 'explain' history by it."[10]

The best hope of speculative history is to present itself as erudite, or otherwise intimidate through its page count and number of footnotes. In the attempt to prove their designs on history, speculative historians marshaled extensive data. H.G. Wells' *The Outline of History*, for example, was first published in four volumes, running to 1,324 pages; A.J. Toynbee's twelve-volume *A Study of History* totaled over 7,000 pages; Oswald Spengler's *The Decline of the West* was first published in German as the 507-page tome *Der Untergang des Abenlandes*; and Thomas Piketty's recent *Capital in the Twenty-First Century*, which while not quite a universal history still speculates a grand law or pattern, comes in at 696 pages.

The shapes of speculative history led its followers to think that the past was quantifiable into discrete chunks that could be organized into patterns, leading to predictive capacity. In other words, chronological structure and periodization can be used argue for a general pattern or purpose of history. Usually the authors have some moral purpose or desire to reshape society along a certain religious or quasi-religious utopian plan. Speculative historians decide on their categories, bend data to fit their scheme, then ignore counter-examples. They largely deny individual agency, or, like Condorcet, think individuals have free well, but their cumulative actions follow statistically demonstrable patterns. Kant used this kind of reasoning to argue that while an individual chooses to get married, marriage rates in his Prussia were subject to stable natural laws.[11] A common progressive view of history combines directionality (progress upwards or forwards) with fixed stages of development from savagery, barbarism, and civilization.

Gordon Graham provides some of the best writing on the philosophy of progress in history. To get at the shape of the past, Graham describes a thought experiment with the Impartial Observer, an ajudicator between historical periods, of a:

> strictly human nature, one that is in no way cultivated by the practices or preferences of any given age, class, or civilization. As a result, their preferences for one age of society rather than another may be said to be a purely human preference, and hence can be regarded as an impartial preference between alternative points in human history.[12]

But even if we were somehow to measure happiness across time, it does not mean that the pattern we see is anything but accidental.

The history profession has not seriously entertained speculative history in a century, yet readership for speculative history remains and its writers are lauded for their insights. Paul Costello reflects on the historical profession's general feeling towards Spengler: "Brilliant as his insights and his manipulations of historical patterns could be, Spengler's scholarship was shoddy, his grasp of the historical record inadequate, and his designs controlled by his guiding ideas."[13] And about Toynbee, Costello is equally unkind: Toynbee "employed *a priori* conclusions" and "mixed metaphors," "concludes from analogies," and "acts as though 'mental reconstructions' are self-evident truths that do not require concrete definition."[14] Likewise, J.W. Swain, reviewing H.G. Wells's *The Outline of History*, states that the book was a "gigantic hoax," and that Wells "merely saw various facts in the past which he wished to string together in the form of a connected narrative" while "his imagination and sympathies did the rest." Swain then hit at the crux of the problem: "Philosophers ever since the days of Hume have been aware that causal relations are never directly observed, but only inferred. Likewise, no clear progress of history has ever been observed by any one; it can only be inferred."[15]

In near unanimity, historians at mid-century rejected as nonsensical mysticism the "speculative" histories imagined by the likes of Oswald Spengler, Arnold Toynbee, and H.G. Wells. In a similar way, professional historians lost faith in all forms of teleological history, whether of the Christian kind in which God's providence directs the course of history, or the Hegelian version, wherein the spirit of reason expresses itself through a historical process. Teleological history in the form of Progressivism also struggled in the wake of the great catastrophes of the twentieth century. Karl Marx's version of history marching inevitably through material stages of production stubbornly held on in some circles, despite its obviously poor record of prediction.

Speculative history was and is attractive precisely because it provides us with useful metaphors. We speak of the present political election as a moment in time, a fulcrum on which the line of history rests. We speak of being on the right side of history. We cannot divorce ourselves entirely from the progressive view or the Christian view or the cyclical view because each is so powerful and useful in ideological rhetoric. But it is also dangerous when we do not recognize the limitations—or even the arbitrary nature—of those metaphors.

The metaphors of speculative history came under attack in mid-twentieth-century debates about the philosophy of history. In previous generations, historians had generally assumed a social scientific bent, and were primarily concerned with determining the quality of data. To establish history as a professional discipline, they distanced themselves from the literary historians of the nineteenth century, men such as Francis Parkman and Jules Michelet, who saw history as a narrative art. Historians came instead to question the very nature of historical knowledge. They viewed methodology as encompassing more than source compilation and criticism. They seriously questioned whether history was a science. Positivist science and speculative history were closely linked in their metaphorical understanding of the past, but the challenges to positivism forced many to abandon speculative history as well.

Stage theories and grand designs of history have been pushed to the margin in academic history, but they flourish in popular culture, especially within religious circles as zealots attempt to predict when the end of days will come. But those who continue to promote speculative history are generally not aware of the philosophical attacks that decimated speculative history in the mid-twentieth century.

Arguments about the Science of Speculation

Science seeks universal patterns, and speculative history proposes that there are such patterns or metaphorical structures in history. The most powerful defender of the "history-as-science" view was Carl Hempel, who in the 1940s proposed that all human behavior could be subsumed under general laws that "covered" all social sciences. History was, in Hempel's view, essentially no different than economics or sociology in that these disciplines were concerned with discovering empirical patterns that could be aggregated to demonstrate fixed relationships or laws of human behavior. No one, however, seemed to be able yet to point conclusively to any historical laws. Inspired by the positivism of August Comte, the Russian historian V.O. Kliuchevskii explained in 1903 that he was looking for these laws, but thought history was too young a science to be able to yet find them.

> We know that historical life and the entire universe must have its own law-governed regularity; a necessary connection of causes and effects. However, the present level of historical science does not enable us to comprehend this connection.[16]

Likewise, in 1941, Edgar Zilsel argued that we would arrive at historical laws through further study, and that the discipline of history was in a beginning stage and had centuries of work to do to catch up to the physicists.[17] To find the patterns in the past, historians argued, we just needed more data. Defenders of this positivist view of history have always admitted that the laws which they are looking for have not been found yet. Given enough data and analysis, however, they were convinced that future historians would discover them. In 1951, S.S. Nilson claimed to have arrived at historical truths that approached the status of historical laws. He presented an absurd view that a claim like "women everywhere vote less frequently than men" is a "universal tendency."[18]

There are simple schemas to explain historical change which fit clear metaphors in our minds, so we want them to be true; we see an aesthetic value in them, even if we know they are incorrect. We are deceived by simple explanations because we can remember them, and because they are aesthetically pleasing. In the back-and-forth of election seasons, we want to make predictions based on the patterns of the past. To guess the next move in a game, or predict the direction of the stock market, we gravitate towards mechanistic, deterministic metaphors for history. But there has long been a school of historical thought that defines history an autonomous discipline, arguing the kind of knowledge it produced was not subject to such "covering laws" and that predictions could only be general and imprecise.[19] The "autonomists," as some have called them, argued that historical knowledge was particular and contextual, arising from an understanding of changes over time. Correlations in certain places and times, they argued, were not really "laws" of universal standing. It is difficult enough, they thought, to figure out cause and effect in the past, let alone apply it to what is going on today or tomorrow. The approach of the autonomists was and is generally to treat history as a score composed by the free, purposive actions of individuals. Rejecting the idea that we can derive historical laws from empirical observation, they do not deny that we can make useful generalizations about the past.[20]

Postivists and Idealists

Different schools of history employ different kinds of metaphors. One possible and convenient way to divide historical schools is into idealist and positivist camps. Economists tend to be attracted to the positivist view of history. Positivists believe regularities in human behavior can be discovered through induction, and that we can establish general laws. Positivists believe that human activity is caused; idealists believe that it is chosen. The idealist tradition developed primarily in Germany, where Wilhelm Windelband decried that "if action is caused, it's not free." Windelband believed that no laws could govern how personalities express themselves. Because if there were actual laws of behavior, then we must by necessity act according to them. If we don't act in such a way, they are not laws.[21] Windelband argued that no matter how many laws of history one has, one could still not explain an individual event.

The views of positivists and idealists can be described in this way:

Positivist	Idealist
progress	historicism (no pattern)
laws/determinism	free will/human action/intention
generalization	uniqueness of events
causes	reasons
explanation	understanding
detachment(objectivity)	empathy
correspondence	coherence

Positivists prefer mechanical metaphors, and they are more likely to see structure in history. Three Austrians—Karl Popper, Ludwig Von Mises, and F.A. Hayek—had already in the 1930s been challenging the view that history is a positive science, that we could discern regular patterns in, or make consistent predictions based on, historical knowledge. Most of their work on the subject came out in the 1950s, however. While the powerful critiques from Mises and Hayek were seldom read by the historians, Karl Popper became a well-known figure in debate about historical knowledge.[22] Popper's *The Poverty of Historicism* presented a view that since we cannot know how scientific knowledge will grow, we cannot predict the course of future events, or create social scientific laws of history.[23] Popper challenged positivism from other angles, as well, by arguing that we cannot confirm the truth of historical statements, but that we can only show them to be false. For Popper, then, we can only work towards historical truth, but not reach it.

Additional arguments helped to put the nail in the coffin of the Hempelian view. In 1960, in a work of resounding impact, Thomas Kuhn challenged scientists to recognize that even scientific observation and theory was subject to historical contingency. With Kuhn in mind, historians could now argue not that history should aspire to be a science, but that scientists could not avoid thinking historically.[24] In a similar attack, in 1965, Arthur Danto argued that a past event could not be understood outside of a narrative relationship between the event and a future condition. No one could say in 1618 that the Thirty Years' War is starting today; nor could a person in 1750 announce that the Industrial Revolution has just begun. Conceptual categories of time are formed after the historical fact. For this reason, Danto contended, history cannot be subject to absolute laws that prescribe meaning prior to seeing events unfold.[25]

With the proposed scientistic foundations of history removed, certainty seemed less likely, and metaphors of structure seemed arbitrary, imposed, even naïve. Many thought that history was sliding closer towards relativism, and historians would need to abandon objectivity as a goal since any such kind of objectivity seemed to entail the denial of moral claims. With important questions solved, or perhaps with the entire field of thought so muddled that these questions could no longer be productively entertained, historians retreated to focus on their craft without all that introspection. The philosophy of history persisted, however, as a kind of fringe subfield, closely tied to postmodernist theory. During the 1970s and 1980s, the focus shifted from questions about the truth of particular statements about the past to the character of narrative statements and text.

Speculative history is no longer in fashion among professional historians, but conspiracy theorists and readers of popular literature still enjoy it. Pounding on the desk, "connecting the dots," they like simple metaphors of circles or lines. This is why I like to tell students about the single conspiracy rule. Let's call it "Douma's Single Conspiracy Rule." I suggest that historians should only be allowed to entertain a single conspiracy theory, and that they do so only as an exercise in understanding the manipulation of sources, logic, and metaphor. So, for the sake of my argument, you may choose one and only one of the following beliefs: 1) The JFK Assassination was directed by the CIA/KGB/Cuba/Lyndon Johnson, 2) Bigfoot/the Loch Ness Monster/Ogopogo walks/swims/crawls amongst us, or 3) Extraterrestrials regularly visit our planet. The problem is, however, that as soon as you truly believe in a single conspiracy theory, your mind stops working like a historian's. You stop critically balancing the evidence, and instead you seek evidence to support your view. When history is a line or a circle, any point in space and time must fit your metaphor. Conspiracy theorists have unmoldable, unquestioned metaphors. When you start accepting conspiracy theories (and I've met plenty of people who simultaneously hold multiple, even contradictory theories), you stop being a historian. If you feel the disrespect of your friends or colleagues who reject your fringe views, you begin to sympathize with others whose own fringe views on other subjects have alienated them from their peers.

Cycles as Metaphor in Speculative History

Cyclical history, as opposed to teleological history, comes in two types. One uses the circle as a metaphor, but might be more accurately described in terms of oscillations of a line or a spiral. These cyclical history theories propose that we can "map" one set of events on top of another. In their view, some fragment of time can be imagined as existing on a timeline, but events of similar nature are when timelines loop back upon themselves. There must be some repetition in life, of the kind of statement like "every day, I drink coffee and get the mail"—but to say that history necessarily repeats itself, or that there is some sociological force at play in larger cyclical patterns, is a different matter. Without an underlying motor, cycle theory is merely a classifying system. The second kind of cyclical view of history is best known in the works of Friedrich Nietzsche and his doctrine of eternal recurrence: If time is infinite, then at some point in the future, all particulars that stand as they do now must return to their present state and history writ large must recur an infinite number of times. Attributed to Nietzsche here is a quote, "All configurations that have previously existed on this earth," Nietzsche wrote, "must yet meet, attract, repulse, kiss, and corrupt each other again . . . and thus it will happen one day that a man will be born again."[26]

Modern leading voices of cyclical history include Peter Turchin and Sergey Nefedov, co-authors of a book titled *Secular Cycles*.[27] Turchin and Nefedov present vast amounts of data to demonstrate supposedly universal, long-term oscillations in pre-industrial agricultural societies. They claim that there are four periods—expansion, stagflation, crisis, and depression—that each agriculture society experiences at the regional level, largely as a result of demographic factors. This argument faces various methodological problems, particularly in the looseness of its definitions. What is a cycle or an oscillation? Are they the same thing? Is any kind of repetition whatsoever a cycle? How do we define the geographical boundaries of a region, or the temporal boundaries of the proposed four period structure? Most historians who look for cycles in history allow the length of these cycles to vary considerably. Similar schemes play fast and loose with the terms "generation" and "civilization," using whatever dates or data makes a convenient fit. If, in Turchin's case, societies evolved out of these cycles, the cycles don't seem so universal or inevitable after all. What I also worry about here is mistaking how people tend to act in particular circumstance with some kind of determinism that says they must or will always act in such a way. Tendencies in historical change are interesting, but such tendencies are not laws and have little predictive power. The historian Jan de Vries makes essentially the same point in his review of Turchin and Nefedov's book: "The predictions only apply to past events, when large agrarian societies and empires were dominant, which is not what most readers will think of as prediction."[28]

One interesting trend in speculative history of this type is that greater and greater amounts of data are needed for increasingly limited claims. Instead of applying such a "science of history" to any small-scale actions or events, writers from Ibn Battuta and Giambattista Vico all the way to the present apply their predictions to the macro level, where it is easier to press some data into the form one seeks to find. They make great promises about unlocking the physical, social, and metaphysical forces that determine the course of history, but fail to deliver much at all. This is not to say that there are no cycles in history. On the contrary, patterns and repetition, even recognizable cycles, are everywhere to be found in the data of the past.

But recognizing that there are simple relationships in society—such that one state of affairs tends to lead to the next—is a far cry from proclaiming that there can be a historical science of prediction. Those who believe that history has cycles or oscillations must first ask: what is oscillating, and what is the oscillator? In other words: what are the particular data that appear to repeat, and what is causing them to repeat? History itself, imagined as some single grand thing, can be neither the cause nor the effect of such repetitions. It is only in particular facts, not all-encompassing overviews, that repetitions are possible, because for something to repeat it needs discrete points that have some attributes that are relative to other discrete points. The old cliché is that those who don't study history are bound to repeat it.[29] Certainly, we can learn from the past, but history never repeats itself exactly.

One of the main problems with metaphors for history is that we can seek any kind of pattern, but the entirety of an event never repeats itself. Data for cycles is seldom of equal kind, it never matches a theory perfectly, and the data is seldom useful in prediction. Certain cycles of crop failures or prices in a stable society can be discovered and explained by climatology or economics and demography, respectively. Dates in history are rarely precise markers or landmarks of change. In dating the fall of the Roman Empire, speculative historians will use whatever date is most convenient to their story.

Pattern-Seeking as a Quasi-Religious Exercise

Speculative history, often paired with numerology and biblical literalism, remains a powerful force in religious views on history. Christianity and Judaism need written history to justify prophecies, and some adherents want to find historical patterns to help predict history's end. Diagrams outlining the coming apocalypse can be powerful in suggesting a new way of seeing time. They appear authoritative when they look official. Diagrams of Christian history are seldom titled "a view on history," but are always made to seem as if there are no other possible interpretations. Diagrams have a way of convincing people of the validity of arguments that they would not accept were these arguments merely verbal.

In each set of data, we can interpret two or more points of information to lead to a another piece of information, or to a final, overall pattern. But all sets of data from the past necessarily fall short of capturing all possible data about the past. Let's say, for example, that you have a set of numbers for a baseball game, like the following:

010101010

You might conclude that the home team will always score one run in every even-numbered inning. The data appear to show regularity, perhaps fixity, some kind of established relationship.

What if, however, we have a separate set of data from the game that shows, instead of the runs per inning, the number of batters who got on base with every appearance at the plate. If a "0" stands for a batter not getting to base, and a "1" stands for a batter indeed getting to base, batting data for the home team might look something like this:

01100, 1000, 000, 00111, 000, 1000, 0100, 1111000, 0010

Now, this set of data is perfectly consistent with the first set of data, but it no longer appears so regular. In fact, it would be quite difficult to see a pattern of inevitability in this set. If someone looks deeps enough, they might find some algorithm to account for this pattern, or, they might leave out numbers or use certain estimation techniques (such as economists do all the time) and arrive as some general explanation. Then, it will become clear that with two sets of data from the same game, a historian might propose two different forms of historical patterns, laws, and inevitability. On some scale, we are always going to find patterns or repetitions in data. If we try hard enough, we can find what appear to be patterns in a random set of numbers, or patterns in text that were not intended to be there.

At the extreme of belief in statistical correlations and numerology we come to such absurdities as "the Bible Code," a view that hidden knowledge of terrestrial events is encoded in the letters of the Bible, or even Anatoly Fomenko's new chronology, the idea that the middle ages never occurred, and our global dating system is wildly inaccurate. If we allow these kinds of ideas to take hold, then anything goes, and we might as well give up on historical chronology altogether. A few hundred years ago, chronology of the ancient world was still very much up for debate. Even Isaac Newton played his hand at this game, with a work titled *The Chronology of Ancient Kingdoms Amended* (1728). Newton, however, by attempting to squeeze the chronology of the ancient Near East into a story that proved the Israelites were the harbingers of the first civilization, lacked a semblance of coherence. He had to collapse time and play tricks with chronology to make the narrative fit. Even for a scientist as renowned at Newton, the data can easily lead us astray, and the complexities of history simplified and translated into data points can sometimes lead us to see patterns that are not truly there.

Conclusion

Our attempts to find patterns can lead us astray. The bigger the dataset, the greater number of theories there are that seem to logically fit. Large-scale laws of history, wrote the German historian Droysen, "could be discovered daily by the dozen" but they would be of the same value as such sayings as "the measure of a people's civilization is its consumption of soap."[30] Droysen seems to be vindicated today, since attempts to find meaningful laws of history in statistical data of the past have failed.[31] It is already difficult enough to find useful patterns in relatively simple games like chess. Imagine, then, how much more complex are the patterns of individual action that create the economy, or the patterns that determine the course of history. Our creativity can lead us astray when we try to apply metaphorical thought to something concrete. We are impressed by approximate isomorphism between historical events and the regular repetition of revolutions around the sun. We can be swayed by the scientific language, believing that "data points" confirm our perspective, while other, potentially more convincing evidence is cast aside as "anecdotal stories." In attempting to create a science of history, it is particularly strange that so many speculative histories depend on matching years to some pattern. Why not months or revolutions of Halley's Comet? Speculative histories align with conspiracy theories and fringe explanations because they are piecing together facts at far distances to support preferred metaphors. We should be careful about using single metaphors to explain all of history.

My skepticism of speculative history and prediction in history comes from the knowledge that we are easily misled, and that two people will likely infer two plausible processes in any set of data. But also, if we interpret everything in terms of a binary, like the rise and fall of civilizations, or the coming and going of generations, it is too easy to discover irrelevant patterns. But things like civilizations and generations, as far as we can say they are more real than imaginary, don't just rise and fall. Civilizations also evolve, fade, renew, merge with other civilizations, and are destroyed and copied. Roman civilization didn't disappear immediately; it "drifted down stream for a long time" says Kenneth Clark.[32] In addition, by what metric should we measure rise and fall? Practitioners of speculative history cannot agree on what they are measuring; nor can they agree on the length of a generation or a civilization. This is because each of them needs to define these things in their own ways to fit their own schematics. History does not only teach us things we can know, it also teaches us that there are many things we cannot know. History humbles the great planners, the demagogues, and those who would predict the future. "History," writes Reinhart Koselleck, "takes place in the anticipation of incompleteness; any interpretation that is adequate to it therefore must dispense with totality."[33]

Notes

1. Michael Shermer, "Patternicity: Finding Meaningful Patterns in Meaningless Noise: Why the Brain Believes Something Is Real When It Is Not" *Scientific American* (December 1, 2008). Patternicity is also known as "apophenia," the tendency to perceive meaningful patterns within random data. www.scientificamerican.com/article/patternicity-finding-meaningful-patterns/, accessed May 28, 2017.
2. Mireca Eliade, *The Myth of the Eternal Return* (Princeton, NJ: Princeton University Press, 1971).
3. Jo Guldi and David Armitage, *The History Manifesto* (Cambridge: Cambridge University Press, 2014).
4. Knox Peden, "What Is to Be Done?" *Los Angeles Review of Books* (February 18, 2015).
5. Pseudoerasmus, "La longue purée," 2014. https://pseudoerasmus.com/2014/11/10/la-longue-puree/, accessed August 22, 2017.
6. Herbert Butterfield, *The Whig Interpretation of History* (New York: W.W. Norton & Company, 1965), 12.
7. Prediction is the unrealized dream of economics, and so it is no surprise that economists join historians in their attempts to find patterns in history. One of the most well-known examples is known as "Kuznets swings," named after the economist Simon Kuznets. Economist Simon Kuznets proposed cycles of 15–25 years, periods of economic growth and decline that were longer than traditional short-term business cycles. But this cycle length is so vague as to be worthless. Why not fourteen years, or twenty-six?
8. In a similar way, we say history will be kind or unkind to a person or an idea. This way, we give history agency, as if it is some kind of acting force.
9. Gordon Graham, *The Shape of the Past* (Oxford: Oxford University Press, 1997), 62–63.
10. Herbert J. Muller, *The Uses of the Past, Profiles of Former Societies* (Oxford: Oxford University Press, 1957), 46.
11. Bruce Mazlish, *The Riddle of History: The Great Speculators from Vico to Freud* (New York: Harper & Row, 1966), 103.
12. Graham, *The Shape of the Past*, 62–63.
13. Paul Costello, *World Historians and Their Goals: Twentieth-Century Answers to Modernism* (DeKalb, IL: Northern Illinois University Press, 1993), 49.
14. Costello, *World Historians and Their Goals*, 93.
15. Joseph W. Swain, "What Is History? V" *The Journal of Philosophy* 20:13 (June 21, 1923), 337–349, specifically 340.
16. Vasily O. Kliuchesvskii, *Pis'ma dnevniki, aforizmy I mysli ob istorii* (Moscow: Nauka, 1968), 288. Cited in John Gonzalez, "In pursuit of a historical tradition: N.A. Rozhkov's "Scientific Laws of History" *Studies in East European Thought* 59 (2007), 309–346, specifically 339.
17. Edgar Zilsel, "Physics and the Problem of Historico-Sociological Laws" *Philosophy of Science* 8:4 (October 1941), 567–579.

18. S.S. Nilson, "Mechanics and Historical Laws" *The Journal of Philosophy* 48:7 (March 29, 1951), 201–211, specifically 202.

19. Perhaps the best description of this kind of historical thought is found in Louis O. Mink's classic article "The Autonomy of Historical Understanding" *History and Theory* 5:1 (1966), 24–47. Briesach contrasts this with the "assimilationist" position of Carl Hempel and Karl Popper. Ernst Breisach, *Historiography: Ancient, Medieval, & Modern* (Chicago: The University of Chicago Press, 1983), 332–335.

20. They see narrative understanding as a crucial historical perspective, separate from scientific explanation. They do not deny empirical observation, but they believe that theory must precede interpretation. Contra Hegel and Marx, they believe that there is no ultimate purpose in history, no logical direction in which it proceeds. They uphold the unique, single historical acts by rational yet imperfect minds. Representatives of this school of thought might be considered to be: Benedetto Croce, *History as the Story of Liberty* (New York: Meridian Books, 1955 [original 1938]); Walter Bryce Gallie, *Philosophy and the Historical Understanding* (New York: Schocken Books, 1964); and Ludwig von Mises, *Epistemological Problems of Economics* (New York: New York University Press, 1976 [original in German, 1933]), 1933. Some of the best works on epistemology of history include William Henry Walsh, *An Introduction to Philosophy of History* (London: Hutchinson House, 1951); William H. Dray, ed., *Philosophical Analysis and History* (New York: Harper and Row Publishers, 1966).

21. David Bebbington, *Patterns in History* (Leicester, England: Inter-Varsity Press, 1979).

22. Ludwig Von Mises, *Theory and History: An Interpretation of Social and Economic Evolution* (New Haven, CT: Yale University Press, 1957). Friedrich A. von Hayek's chapter "The Historicism of the Scientistic Approach" in *The Counter-Revolution of Science: Studies on the Abuse of Reason* (Indianapolis, IN: Liberty Fund, 1979 [1952]).

23. Karl Popper, *The Poverty of Historicism* (London: Routledge and Kegan Paul, 1957). Popper's greatest legacy might be his redefinition of the word "historicism." It can truly be said that there are at least two dogmas of historicism. On the one hand, in nineteenth-century Germany, historicism meant simply an attachment to the sources as evidence of unique events. In the original conception, historicists were those who believed historical data could not be used to accurately predict the future. Popper turns the term upside-down by making the historicists those who believe in patterns of history. The best writing on historicism is clearly Friedrich Beiser, *The German Historicist Tradition* (Oxford: Oxford University Press, 2006).

24. Thomas Kuhn, *The Structure of Scientific Revolutions* (Chicago: University of Chicago Press, 1962).

25. Arthur C. Danto, *Narration and Knowledge, Including the Integral Text of Analytical Philosophy of History* (New York: Columbia University Press, 1985 [original 1965]). Reinhart Koselleck has defended a similar view that our conceptual periodization must precede our research into the sources. Reinhart Koselleck, *The Practice of Conceptual History: Timing History, Spacing Concepts* (Stanford, CA: Stanford University Press, 2002).

26. Walter Arnold Kaufmann, *Nietzsche: Philosopher, Psychologist, Antichrist* (Princeton, NJ: Princeton University Press, 1974), 318.

27. Peter Turchin and Sergey A. Nefedov, eds., *Secular Cycles* (Princeton, NJ and Oxford, UK: Princeton University Press, 2009).

28. Jan De Vries, "Review of *Secular Cycles* by Peter Turchin and Sergey A. Nefedov" *Population Studies* 64:2 (July 2010), 203–204.

29. I prefer the saying that "those who don't study history are bound to repeat my class."

30. Johann Gustav Droysen, "The Elevation of History to the Rank of a Science: Being a Review of *The History of Civilization in England* by H.T. Buckle" (original

1861) in Johann Gustav Droysen, ed. *Outline of the Principles of History* (translated by E. Benjamin Andrews) (New York: Howard Fertig, 1967).

31. For examples of attempts to find cycles of human behavior, see: John T. Burns, *Cycles in Humans and Nature: An Annotated Bibliography* (Metuchen, NJ: The Scarecrow Press, 1994). If any of the cycles proposed were useful or relevant, many would have found ways to predict them in the future and profit from them.

32. Kenneth Clark, *Civilizations* (London: BBC and John Murray, 1971), 4.

33. Koselleck, *The Practice of Conceptual History*, 23–24.

12 Useful Diagrams Have Specific, Not General, Aims

Diagrams of history should not attempt to seek ultimate explanatory power, but rather should focus in on a few key relationships that they wish to explain and explore. One of my own designs is a triangle diagram of history, archeology, and journalism (Figure 12.1). The diagram represents how scholars in these three disciplines interact with evidence. A historian wants neither too few nor too many facts. An archeologist stands on the extreme end, with few facts to work with. She might unearth a single pottery shard and write a dissertation about it. A student of contemporary affairs, on the other end, will sift through mountains of data to craft a thesis of comparable length. The archeologist likely expands upon a small set of sources, whereas journalists and modern historians condense a pile of sources to form their arguments. Most historians operate along the spectrum somewhere between archeologists and journalists. The nineteenth century, I would argue, is the "sweet spot" for historians: there are neither too few sources (as in many cases is true for research on the eighteenth century and before), nor too many sources (such as in our data-driven twenty-first century.) In addition, documents from the nineteenth century are still in physical form (as opposed to today's digital photography, for example), the papers from that era are generally legible, the culture is recognizable, and the struggles of the people quite understandable. Go back another century and there is a greater cultural, political, and linguistic divide separating the past from the present that makes it more like we are studying a foreign people.

At some point in the distant past, we essentially run out of factual information and can only make informed guesses as to what was going on. Archeology is traditionally concerned with the prehistoric period, in which there are no written records of civilizations. I have a lot of respect for archeologists, but I still find it funny that they can know so little about a group of people that they must define them by the form of pottery they left behind. In a tautology, the discovery of ancient clay beakers will lead to the establishment of an entire civilization called the "beaker culture" people. Likewise, anthropologists who can't find a clear purpose for some historical artifact might say that it has "ritual use," as if that has any meaning at all. At any rate, the line between archeology and history represents the transition to the written record, and with it, an expansion in the number of sources available. As we move to the

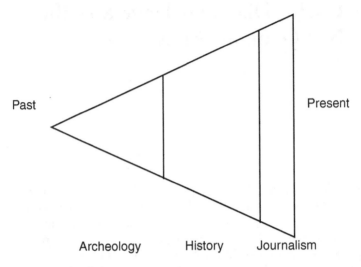

Past   Present

Archeology   History   Journalism

Figure 12.1 Triangle of History

Douma's triangle diagram of history. On the x-axis is the historical time under study from ancient on the left, to modern on the right. The height of the diagram represents the total number of sources or facts available to the researcher studying a period in the past.

right of the diagram, towards the present days the number of possible sources grows exceedingly large, so that the best we can hope for is an interpretation of a viable cross-section of the relevant data.

This diagram also reflects the view that journalists are, in a way, front-line historians, reporting on the facts that others will later use for chronicle and history. Journalists must produce material quickly and are naturally less concerned with ultimate truth than is an archeologist or historian. This might explain why archeology journalism tends to be so poor, even though it doesn't have to be. This is because the journalist wants a catchy headline with an immediate insight, whereas the archeologist knows that knowledge reveals itself gradually through careful thought. Archeologists are patient and avoid rushing to conclusions. For the most part, they are not really interested in contemporary journalism. Journalists, on the other hand, are brokers of facts; they buy and sell information, whether it be true or false. Journalists work fast, historians work a bit slower.

Well-written history, I believe, needs to take a moderate position between these two approaches. History must be concerned with events sufficiently deep in the past so that the long-term consequences of actions can be understood. It is very difficult to write the history of something that happened only twenty years ago, especially if the subject is very large and the effects are still being felt directly. There are plenty of proverbs about a wise man in the modern Middle East, who, when he was asked, "What are the consequences of the Crusades?" answered: "It is too soon to tell." Until a story unfolds, until its long-term consequences can be seen, we cannot understand the complete meaning of an event. History is the opposite of current events. To think like a historian, you cannot be bombarded by the daily news, the distractions of the present, the short-term trends which pull your mind from seeing patterns over geologic time.

History as a Supra-Discipline

If you spend a career working in one discipline, you begin to see the world like others around you. You use the same language to describe things, the same metaphors to understand cause and effect. Over time, many people become wedded to the ideas of their discipline and cannot see the world through any other lens.

From time to time, I encounter economists who say that they are thankful that there are historians out there in the world, because historians are necessary to find the data that economists use to interpret human behavior. There is this widespread idea among various social scientists that history is merely a discipline of content, not theory or understanding, and that the real thinking ought to be left to non-historians. This is an old conceit. J.W. Swain, writing in 1923, complained that:

> in recent years many [Sociologists] have endeavored to show that the historian's task is to collect data upon which they may base their general theories. History for them would be what the laboratory is to the chemist: history would become the handmaiden of sociology.[1]

To counter such disciplinary snobbery, I like to tell social scientists about a pyramid of disciplines as historians see it. In my mental pyramid of the disciplines, I naturally place history at the top. Lower blocks on the pyramid include economics, sociology, political science, literature, even natural science—all of the other disciplines that can contribute to historical understanding and that historians draw on from time to time to explain the world. From this perspective, history is at the top because it uses or can use knowledge from all other disciplines. The social sciences are self-constrained, use models, and aim for replication—but history is open to exploring more broadly. History is, in fact, a supra-discipline, and we can envision it as a comprehensive study of everything empirical and theoretical. It is not focused on just one topic. The Italian polymath Benedetto Croce wrote that: "Historical knowledge is not a variety of knowledge, but it is knowledge itself; it is the form which completely fills and exhausts the field of knowing."[2] The philosopher J.W. Swain took an equally charitable view of the scope of historical knowledge:

> The natural sciences all have very clearly defined subjects with which they deal: thus botany deals with plants, zoology with animals, chemistry with the constitution of matter, and so forth. But history does not have any such distinctive field. It deals with men and institutions, with society.[3]

This fits in to an interesting and old, unsettled debate about whether history is a science or an art. In nineteenth-century American history, writing was thought to be a popular form of literary consumption, much more like an art than a science. Historians like Parkman, Prescott, and Motley wrote tomes that were bestsellers. Historians in this period were concerned with sources, but they also wanted to tell a good story. This present book is partially an attempt to recover that old view that sees a personal, creative element at play in historical writing. It was in the later part of the nineteenth century, as history became professionalized and as history was added to the university curriculum, that the discipline began to have the pretensions of a science. A science, however, needs laws and a body of knowledge that is consistent and applicable. This confusion is all the greater because in the English language we treat "science" as a term co-equal with natural sciences, and with empirical observation more particularly. In German, however, the term *Wissenschaft* means something more broad, and often this German conception gets brought into the discussion.

In the past century, physics, not history, has often been imagined to be resting at the top of the academic pyramid. "Physics envy" affected the social sciences first, but history (which may be a social science or a humanity, depending on how you look at it) quickly followed suit. Because of the precision of physics, and the success of its theories for predicting and discovering new things, every other discipline wanted to be more scientific, more like the physicists. The discipline of history has long had a pretension towards scientific prediction, but was ultimately happy to rely on scientific exactitude as disciplinary ethic, rather than scientific law as an object of its pursuit.

I don't know if my pyramid diagram is a true description of the relationship between disciplines, or if indeed the category of true and false really applies here, since it is a perceptual observation I am making, not a truth claim. At any rate, a pyramid diagram with history at the top is useful to lampoon the pretensions of other disciplines, but also helps to show others how historians believe their work is important.[4] We have tried the rule of elites (aristocracy), the rule of the people (democracy), and even the rule by religion (theocracy). If historians are at the top of the pyramid, perhaps it is time for society to be run by historians (histocracy).

Historical vs. Longitudinal Diagram

Of course, different diagrams are necessary to explain history for different audiences. In explaining the historical method to colleagues in the field of organizational management, R. Daniel Wadhwani uses an ingenious set of images designed to contrast the historical method with the longitudinal and cross-sectional analysis types common to business school scholarship (Figure 12.2). In cross-sectional study, one observer at one moment in time makes a number of observations. In a longitudinal study, a number of observers each makes a similar observation but at different times. In historical study, on the other hand, a researcher links different kinds of observations made by a variety of

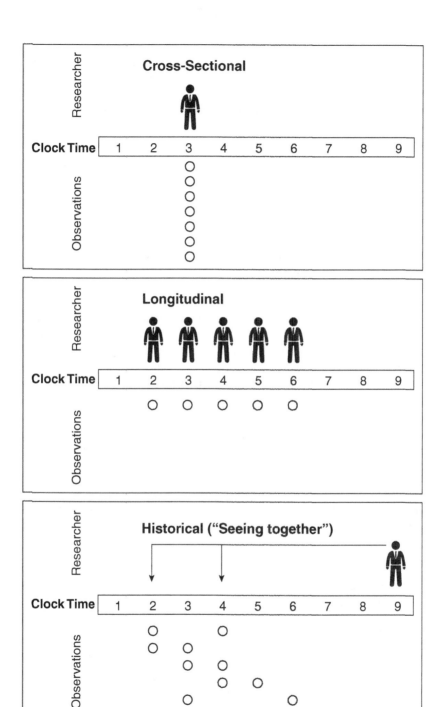

Figure 12.2 History vs. Social Science

A series of diagrams, based on those by R. Daniel Wadhwani, to show how the historical method differs from other social scientific scholarship.

people. Wadhwani takes the example a step further by explaining that in the historical method, the observations are not made directly, but are taken from sources. By seeking patterns in these historical observations, a researcher proposes conceptual structures or stages reflecting changes over time.[5]

Sometimes the simplest diagrams are the most useful and convincing, but not necessarily the most accurate. A good example of this is a Venn diagram with one circle labeled "all possible true historical knowledge" and second, much smaller circle, falling mostly inside the larger circle and labeled "what we know about history." The trouble with this common diagram is that the concept of *all* possible historical knowledge would include such an incredibly large array of information as to absolutely dwarf the second circle. It would include the names of all the pet cats in twelfth-century Burgundy, all freight rates in imperial China, and the mental motivations of every hunter and gatherer. We kid ourselves when we think we know so much. Historians might be able to explain some large patterns of history, but they cannot pretend to know 1 percent of 1 percent of all possible historical facts. Even if we had a device to view the past directly, like Asimov's fictional neutrino-detecting chronoscope, we still wouldn't be able to explain all of history. We can't see the motivations inside people's heads. We can't explain all possible arrangements, or rhythm and relationships between all matter.

Reflecting for a moment on this diagram, we might even want to challenge the idea that there is such a thing as "the set of all true historical facts." Is there a finite amount of historical knowledge; does it have some boundary? I would suggest that there is no limit to the number of potential historical facts, since each perspective we take on the past gives us new relationships to consider. That is to say, there is no "all of the events that ever happened," but only perspectives on them. History is not an accumulation of stuff, but an interpretation of it. We can always find new ways to arrange the facts to find new meanings. It is as if someone were to say that we can know all possible songs, all possible combinations of all possible notes.

Notes

1. Joseph W. Swain, "What Is History?" *The Journal of Philosophy* 20:11 (May 24, 1923), 281–289, specifically 282.
2. Benedetto Croce, *History as the Story of Liberty* (Indianapolis, IN: Liberty Fund, 2000 [original English version London: Allen & Unwin, 1941]), 30.
3. Swain, "What Is History?," 282.
4. Such a pyramid diagram, of course, is not the only way to envision the array of academic discipline. For centuries, academics in the Western world spoke of the seven liberal arts, consisting of a trivium (represented by a triangle): grammar, rhetoric, and logic; and a quadrivium (represented by a square): mathematics, geometry, astronomy, and music. Above these seven were philosophy and theology.
5. Rohit Daniel Wadhwani, "Historical Knowledge in Business & Management: A Case of Academic Entrepreneurship." PowerPoint slides from the author.

13 Analogies of Historical Thinking

Ask students to compare & contrast historians with musicians, detectives, lawyers (& lawyers, detectives, ...)

This second chapter of Section IV argues that to see history as a creative discipline, it can be useful to think of history itself in metaphorical terms, comparing it to other subjects like music, law, and science. While speculative history is an abuse of metaphor for ideological purpose, comparisons of history to other disciplines are useful, non-ideological ways of explaining the historical method. History is not really all that different from other disciplines, and the overlap in their methods highlights grounds for cooperation and mutual understanding. Historians, I believe, are like musicians, detectives, lawyers, and scientists.

Historians Are Like Musicians

More than any other analogy, I think that viewing the course of history as a musical score offers a useful way of understanding the creative historical mind.

We all have some historical sense, just like we all have some musical sense. Even if you have not formally studied music, you are able to recognize musical patterns and structures in a song. Nothing demonstrates this fact more clearly than our response when a song is played poorly, or when a song is cut short. Think back to a time when you were listening to a song in the car or perhaps on your computer, and the song was interrupted. Maybe your friend turned off the radio before the song was finished, or the computer froze up. We have all experienced this at one point or another, and for many of us it was a deeply frustrating experience. The reason why it was frustrating is because our minds are actively seeking structure. When the song ended prematurely, you knew or at least anticipated that there were another few notes or a verse to follow. This sense of music indicates that you hear more than just individual notes—you also abstract patterns, and you recognize melodies. Notes form a song, but a song has structure in measures and verses.

In history as well, there are short-term themes, and themes over the long term, periods defined by a decade or so and epochs defined by centuries of time. Developments over the *longue durée*, as they say in the French "Annales" school of history, are difficult to observe.

There is not one set of historical events, but many, happening at the same time. These occur at geological, social, and individual paces. This idea appears also in Michael Stanford's view that "historical phenomena occur in short, medium, and long cycles, interweaving and overlapping like tunes in a Bach fugue."[1] This perspective may even extend past metaphor and analogy. Certainly, the part of the brain responsible for music and the part responsible for memory are connected. Greeks sang the *Odyssey* and other epics to help them remember the past; Gregorian chant connected oral history and written history with notated music. With the development of musical notation, written records of music and stories could reinforce and help preserve oral traditions. Musical notation is the process of translating sound waves to scaled dots on horizontal lines. History is a written record(ing) of the past.

Contemporary history is difficult to analyze because we cannot always hear the longer rhythms of the past. While the French Annales school wants to emphasize the long term, it does not neglect the shorter patterns. This is why the time element is so crucial to the historical method. Unlike scientific observation, historians cannot create data and then immediately put it to use. Developments occur in context. Historians create historical ages, periods, and epochs by dividing the flow of time into discrete units—but each hears the melody in a different way, and may choose to break up the song at a different point.

Historians are like musicians who are aware of the invisible but underlying patterns in song. As I argued in chapters two and three, historians are not in the business of just memorizing facts. You wouldn't say that a musician just knows how to recognize or play notes. Instead, a musician puts notes in order and creates melodies with them. Musicians bring order to sound. Historians, on the other hand, bring order to historical facts—they explain change and elucidate cause and effect. Historians do not just repeat information, but rather they arrange it in creative ways. In short, historians write narratives the way musicians write songs. Facts are like notes, stories are like melodies, and essays are like songs to the historian. This isn't my first book, but because the ideas in this book are more personal than the material in my other books, it feels like my debut album.

Good historical writing is like a symphony played by a well-formed orchestra. All the sources (instruments) have come together at one time to form a logical whole. The sources reinforce each other and work together towards a common goal, but the pattern is subtle and the conductor considers small variations and nuances.

Others have noticed the parallels between history and music. The theologian Gordon Clark, for example, uses a musical analogy to show how the limitations of empirical observation might cause historians to construct false views of a past event:

One may compare the historical narrator with a man listening to an organist playing an intricate work on five keyboards. This man is recovering from defective hearing. At the moment he can hear only one note in a hundred, and he reports to us that the organist is playing *My Country, Tis of Thee* with one finger. Although these simple notes may have sounded in their proper order, further recovery of the historian's hearing will alter his narrative."[2]

Clark, an arch anti-empiricist, doubts that historians ever hear the notes in their proper form, and concludes that they are thus incapable of recording the past accurately. But although we might recognize that no musician's ear is perfect, we would not deny the existence of music, stop playing it, or stop enjoying it. Historians or musicians who demand perfection in their craft will never finish their work.

The best historians analyze and write with the same creativity and care as a violinist who has learned to make a violin weep.[3] Chroniclers (those who only list facts in chronological order without analysis), on the other hand, are like player-pianos. Facts without analysis are like notes without emotion, repeated but not felt. Scientists and social scientists who believe that they deal only with facts and not stories should be reminded of this analogy. Economists, for example, also tell stories, but as Deirdre McCloskey reminds us, "much of what they do is history in another key."[4]

Some historians are like cover artists, just reproducing songs, or rewriting the same stories, maybe in a slightly different meter or key. The biography of Abraham Lincoln is an old standby, always open for reinterpretation, a historical work that is so oft-repeated in form that it is like a folk song in which each new performer adds his or her own new lines. The best historians, I believe, certainly know the old stories (as the best musicians can also play classic songs) but they also write new stories, that is, new historical narratives on themes and events that other creative minds had never considered worthy of historical treatment. Two historians using the same facts can write two different—even contradictory—histories, just like musicians using the same notes or working in the same tradition can write two drastically different songs.

Bad history, meanwhile, is noise. Bad historians are like talentless musicians who don't have rhythm and don't produce anything new, but rather only like to hear themselves play. The remedy for bad history is not necessarily more memorization of a larger number of facts. Historical facts are necessary to form a story, and musical notes are necessary to form a song, but neither facts nor notes are as pleasing on their own as they are when they are creatively arranged in interesting patterns. That is to say, until they are put in order, until they make sense, facts are historical noise. This distracting noise posing as history can be found in many forms. Current events are the most prevalent kind of noise which distracts historians. Listening to the news is like listening to a sample track of a bunch of songs getting cut off before they finish playing. Or better yet, listening to the media report current events is like listening to an explosion of notes from a variety of songs, a wave of static noise, with no way to tell where these notes came from or where they belong. Data is just noise until the signal is decoded. Historical noise is present in every published article in which there are facts but no argument or analysis. Historical noise exists every time a propagandist or dogmatist drills facts into the minds of their captives. Historical noise fills textbooks, television, and the Internet. It takes patience, concentration, and a clear mind to listen to the past.

Historians Are Like Detectives

There was a day not too long ago when everyone wanted to become a forensics expert. Crime shows on television convinced us that young, attractive, super-intelligent people were everywhere solving murders. Since the evening news told us that murders were quite frequent, it seemed to us young folk growing up in the 1990s that it was fairly inevitable that a good number of us would be working as detectives. But by the time we entered college, our dreams were dashed. "Forensics 101" was nowhere to be found in the course catalog, and monster.com did not return any search results for "crime scene investigator." It turned out that in the real world, the demand for detectives was not really so high after all and that the ranks of detectives were more than sufficiently filled by hardened police veterans with tenure. Our dreams shattered, we became English majors so we could write pieces on generational angst for online magazines.[5]

A few of us disenchanted detectives discovered, however, that another name for "detective" is "historian," and that to become one, all we had to do was take a course called "historical methods." In the end, for those of us who wanted to become forensics experts, the closest realistic job option was, in fact, "historian." The historical mysteries needing to be solved were seldom murders, and the solutions didn't always come to us in some late-night revelation, as they also do in a television montage. In the lives of historians, there is too seldom a romantic subplot. But we historians do get paid to travel to remote places, and sometimes we are interviewed as experts. And while some of us may have lamented not seeing the crime scene firsthand, we were generally relieved to look at old papers in an air-conditioned archive, a thousand miles and a hundred years after the battle. We became satisfied with the thought that we had done something constructive.

Historical detective work takes patience and hard work. Like detectives, historians must know how to uncover information that is not spelled out for them in front of their faces. They must master many skills to be successful. It may be a particular language which holds the key to understanding the documents of a community the historian wishes to study. The best historical works solve problems or look at topics in ways that other historians had never imagined. Just as a detective cannot procure a warrant without some evidence or secure a conviction without strong evidence, a historian cannot begin an argument without strong sources or stand by an argument without presenting a thorough case.

A historian-detective needs to think creatively about where evidence might be. A historian can interview someone to get eyewitness information, sift through dirt to find pottery shards in an archeological dig, climb a tower to document historic graffiti, use a microscope to determine the age of a material, or measure the dimensions of historic structures to see how the built environment changed over time. No historian-detective can solve a case by sitting in the library alone. A good detective must be skeptical of third-person testimony, just like a historian must be suspicious of books written by others. Good historical detectives must travel, conduct research, and interact with a variety of people. They must also take advantage of technology. Detectives perceive subtle changes and know, like historians, that any information might be important information for solving the case. A fact might seem a trivial detail at first, but it can become relevant when other information is acquired. Historians and detectives have curiosity to spare.

Because the task of a detective is so well known, the historian-as-detective metaphor is exceptionally useful in history classrooms. Jeffrey Nokes explains:

> By framing an activity as a historical mystery and positioning students as history detectives, they can, with relative ease, adopt an epistemic stance that more closely approximates that of a historian. Similarly, teachers can position students as jurors who interact with evidence about a historical situation in order to render a justifiable verdict.[6]

The popular historian podcaster Dan Carlin uses a similar metaphor when he says that historians are like arson investigators: they know the final result, but not what happened at the scene.

By framing a historical research project as a detective story, a historian can appeal to the universal desire to find resolution to a mystery. Some of the best historical writing approaches its topic by asking a "who done it?" type of question. In a masterful tale in *The Atlantic*, Ariel Sabar asked whether a reference to "Jesus' wife" on an ancient scrap of papyrus could have been faked. Sabar then documents his travels and interviews, outlining the steps of his research and the twists that developed as he worked his way to an answer.[7] Who was the man found dead on the beach of Somerton, Australia in 1948? Who was D.B. Cooper, the alias of the only successful airline hijacker in history? How did the Norse disappear from fifteenth-century Greenland? These kinds of questions drive interest in historical research and help us to get in the mode of trying to figure out the events of the past.

Historians Are Like Lawyers

When looking for evidence, a historian is like a detective, but when presenting evidence, a historian is like a litigation lawyer. Both derive arguments from evidence, describe what they think happened, and try to convince others to agree with them. Lawyers are historians who specialize in modern legal problems. Their archives consist of file folders at the police station. Common law precedent is their historiography. Black letter law—the foundational aspects of law generally free from disputes—is only part of the knowledge lawyers can draw on. Historians, as well, are shaped by procedural process and by a common stock of ideas about how the world works. Law, like history, recognizes competing narratives, in which adversaries argue for the best interpretation.

If you think like a lawyer, you will be a better historian. First of all, it will help you remember that your goal is not simply to accumulate evidence or to restate previous decisions, though those may be relevant tasks when working towards the larger goal. In criminal law, the defendant is guilty or not guilty, and it is the job of the lawyer to argue which one is the case. But most types of law do not result in verdicts that declare one side completely guilty or innocent. In property law, a person may compromise on a right-of-way, and in commercial law, two parties might bargain for an acceptable resolution. Likewise, historical research often leads historians to take a middle ground, to see the story from many perspectives and arrive at a compromise between competing views.

A historian may begin by questioning whether or not Napoleon had a significant impact on the rise of nationalism in Europe. On the surface, this seems like a "yes/no" question. But, the historian might discover, for example, that Napoleon had only a minor impact on the rise of nationalism. A nuanced, balanced presentation can still be persuasive, and is in fact probably more persuasive than a clear, one-sided view. As a historian, you cannot present half of a case, make an ambiguous charge, or claim that the problem is too complicated to be understood. You must state the defendant's plea up front; that is, your thesis must appear in the first few pages. Do not wait until the conclusion to present your position; do not wait till the end of the day to tell the jury that the defendant is not guilty. The jury is your audience. They may be other professional historians, and they may know more than you do, especially if you fail to do your research.

Written legal decisions are like published articles in peer-reviewed journals. Established historians, like established lawyers, become judges as they review arguments submitted to journals. Smaller journals that cover narrow topics are like circuit courts, with limited jurisdiction. But the most established history journals, like the *American Historical Review* or the *Journal of Modern History*, are analogous to the Supreme Court for historians. One difference between the world of the historian and the world of the lawyer, however, is that historians may bring their case to many academic courts. There is double jeopardy in history; you can try someone twice. So, if a historian's article is rejected by one journal, they may send it to another. Academic peer review is a relatively decentralized or polycentric judicial system, and while it certainly has its problems and fair share of corrupt judges, that is, entrenched myopic editorial boards, it also functions like a reasonable legal system, with norms of behavior and expectations. Well-established historical arguments are currency in historians' discourse. Historians cite Alfred Young, Carlo Ginzburg, and E.P. Thompson, or other established historians the way a civil rights lawyer might cite Brown v. Board of Education or Roe v. Wade.

The evidence is sometimes contradictory and does not all point in the same direction. Lawyers who want to convince the jurors of their position must choose to address the issues that the jurors are most concerned with. Similarly, historians must respond to the interests of their colleagues or the reading public if they wish to have an impact. Historians must respect the precedent of established arguments, but challenge them when need be. They must follow the procedural rules of the historian's court, speak loudly and clearly without droning on, greet the judge and jury with a tip of the hat, consult with fellow experts, and be honest in their judgment, lest they be judged.

Historians Are Like Scientists (Kind of)

Historians suffer from physics envy, and they have long pondered whether the discipline of history is a science or an art. If it is a science, then, like other sciences, it ought to have a set of laws, and an established body of knowledge. If history is more like art, though, historians should be seen as creative figures constructing stories to fit their fancy. If history is scientific and useful, historians should get paid like scientists, but if it is like an art, we worry, we will be paid like starving artists. A further confusion enters this conversation whenever the German word for science, *Wissenschaft*, is introduced, because it means both knowledge and science, and the Germans use the term much more broadly. Without solving the old question here and now, we can at least consider how historians think in many ways that parallel the thought processes of scientists.

History is often reported about as if it were a science with predictive capabilities. History, it is often said, is useful for the present, so the written history of one thing or another is carried through right up to the present. A pundit tells their audience what is bound to happen next. In every move by every president, a historian somewhere finds a parallel in the past and publishes an op-ed on the topic. But finding parallels between two anecdotes would never pass as science, and without seeing history from a distance, we can't see how something unfolds. Even scientific experiments can be difficult to replicate perfectly in the lab. Historians must study the themes of the past over and over again to understand them, but good historians are not in the prediction game. Historians and scientists may have a good idea about what comes next, but certainty is elusive.

Knowledge in the scientific community starts as a hypothesis, and this has to withstand intensive testing through experiments before it is established as scientific law. Even then, scientific law is not quite ultimate truth, since empirical claims cannot be proven to be perfectly reliable. At best, science can provide strong trends between variables that indicate strong enough correlations to establish a fixed relationship. What scientists call laws are quite similar to what historians consider established historical facts. Historical facts, however, are particular, unique, and cannot always be applied to explain other circumstances. There is always the chance that something could be discovered later that might dislodge a scientific fact or a historical fact from its status as a "true" fact.

Bad science can happen when lab results are intentionally skewed, or when people ignore or don't fully investigate anomalies in test results. The published reports can then mislead other researchers, or the public more generally. Historians can become similarly disreputable if they allow their desire for particular results or narratives to motivate their validation of their findings.

Good historians, like good scientists, must remind themselves that their findings are not necessarily universal truths. Historians test facts. History, unlike science, does not suggest reproducibility in the lab, but footnotes in historical works do intend to allow other historians to run the same experiment, or at least look at the same materials. Historical facts deemed unimportant or unwanted, although still available, generally fade into obscurity. In this way, the process of historical fact selection is similar to natural selection; the facts that have properties suitable for the historian will be retold, while others will be discarded and fade into the annals of historical purgatory. It may be more appropriate to call this process historical eugenics, as it is not natural selection by true definition; it is the artificial selection on behalf of the historian. History, like science, is a search for understanding, in which theories must withstand challenges. Conclusions about historical figures can be revised, pending discoveries of new evidence.

Notes

1. Michael Stanford, *A Companion to the Study of History* (Malden, MA: Blackwell, 1997 [original 1994]), 17.
2. Gordon H. Clark, *Historiography: Secular and Religious* (Nutley, NJ: Craig Press, 1971), 142.
3. An interesting related point is in: Margaret Boden, "Creativity and Unpredictability" SEHR, volume 4, issue 2 (1995): Constructions of the Mind. Margaret Boden, a leading scholar of creativity, suggests that we can visualize musical space to understand the mind of a musical genius like Mozart. By mapping or plotting structural features of songs, we can see the landmarks that Mozart used to "navigate and negotiate" his musical world.
4. Donald (Deirdre) N. McCloskey, *If You're So Smart: The Narrative of Economic Expertise* (Chicago: The University of Chicago Press, 1990).
5. A good compilation of interesting and unique historical detective work is Robin W. Winks' *The Historian as Detective: Essays on Evidence* (New York: Harper & Row, 1968). A modern work that looks at more common classroom themes and integrated historical methods is James West Davidson and Mark Hamilton Lytle, *After the Fact: The Art of Historical Detection* (Boston: McGraw-Hill, 1992).
6. Jeffrey D. Nokes, *Building Students' Historical Literacy: Learning to Read and Reason with Historical Texts and Evidence* (London: Routledge, 2012), 60.
7. Ariel Sabar, "The Unbelievable Tale of Jesus's Wife" *The Atlantic* (July/August 2016). www.theatlantic.com/magazine/archive/2016/07/the-unbelievable-tale-of-jesus-wife/485573/, accessed July 19, 2016.

14 Creative Historical Thinking for Everyone

In this book, I have argued that creative historical thinking is an attitude of openness and play. It is a view that history should be personal, contentious, up for debate, and ever-present. History should never claim complete certainty or shut down conversation.

History writing is partly an attempt to communicate our perceptions of the past to others. But all too often, we assume that other people are using the exact same conceptual system; we assume that if they are given all the same information we have, they will come to the same conclusions that we did. Instead, in explaining history and trying to convince someone of your particular view, it is probably more important to explain your framework, your way of perceiving the world, than it is to outline the facts of the matter as you see them. When we recognize that other people see the world in different ways, we can better translate our thoughts and communicate them. History is a communicative, cooperative exercise.

Because we cannot observe the past directly, we have to understand it by references to what we know in the present. For this reason, historical knowledge is always tentative, a best guess from the available data. We use metaphors, based on our experiences, to provide models to explain data. Metaphors are comparisons used to get at the essence of the subject in question. We are hard-wired to recognize primary metaphors. To make sense of the data of the past, we often need multiple metaphors and the creativity to apply them in new ways. In looking for metaphors to describe the past, we are limited by the extent of our experiences. There can be no exhaustive set of metaphors, nor can there be a complete demonstration of how they are applied. We don't all speak the same language, but we can still try to understand each other.

We impart history with meaning when we create it to accord with our senses, but we do ourselves a disservice when we end the conversation and close ourselves down to further reinterpretation. Facts are the building blocks of history, but by themselves they tell us very little. We can make sense of historical facts only relative to our position or perspective.

Our initial views of historical developments are simple, clean, and one-directional. As we read more history and research it in archives, we become aware of the messiness and nuance of it all, of the paths that cross over each other and turn back upon one another. The narratives we write are like paths in the wilderness. Each historian blazes their own trail. Historiography is the general direction of historical views about a subject. It is the process of seeing how narrative paths intersect.

We should not be saddened or frustrated to recognize that there is more than one path through the woods. There can be no total, complete history. We should instead be excited by the possibility that each person can discover history for themselves, alone or with others, through books or primary sources, through genealogy or archeology or whatever they encounter when they open an old shoe box found in the attic.

A Way Forward for Creativity

If history is to be reconceptualized as a creative discipline, we have a long way to go. At present, there is a great divide between what students learn in class and what practitioners of the subject actually do. Students in K–12 education never learn about the existence of archives, have little or no sense of primary sources, and generally have a single nationalist narrative pounded into their heads. It is difficult work to create new lessons for every day of the week, and so for the sake of efficiency, teachers rely on the standby of information-soaked textbooks and lectures. Meanwhile, tests support passive learning and memorization. In graduate school, meanwhile, too much is at stake to allow experimentation with new methods of scholarship. Nothing will stop someone from being creative more effectively than the fear of making a mistake and incurring the disapproval of his or her advisor. Evaluation serves as a threat, constantly checking the freedom of creative experimentation. It goes without saying that the sorting process requires that history professors have "completed" their training by making it through all of the levels of schooling. Original and creative thinkers might not have the patience to make it through the system. The hiring process, as well, favors "safe" historians with clear, recognizable teaching and research agendas.

The restrictions in academia have led to a form of false creativity, in which young historians have to pose as experts in everything. Newly minted Ph.D.'s on the market don't need to convince themselves—they just need to convince someone else that they can teach a particular course. They may have only taken one class on the Vietnam War or taught one course on Modern America, but if there is a job opening for a historian of the Vietnam War and they need a job, then by God, they are going to apply for it. I know people who, on paper, have mastered all subjects. They are willing to teach a course on how Karl Barth would interpret Freud in a postmodernist hostage negotiation. They can teach this as a freshman seminar, senior seminar, or senior bingo league lecture. Ironically, it is the death of creativity that lies at the root of this proliferation of phony expertise. Those who are stubbornly creative might find that they have written a dissertation about business in the 1920s, and that this year, there are no positions on the market calling for business historians or historians of the 1920s.

Creative historical thinking should begin in the classroom. For creativity to flourish in history education, we should have fewer classes on historical content and more classes in historical methods and theory, writing, research skills, and cooperative historical projects. A constant theme of these classes should be "doing" history—becoming active, practicing historians by engaging with sources and reading for background to solve problems. In K–12 education, this might mean an increased emphasis on participatory exercises, games, field trips, group work, and other activities that teach history as an interpretative act, and less time spent trying to satisfy the testing bureaucracy. Creative historical thinking in undergraduate education should begin with a course in history methods and approaches to history, which should precede any general survey course. In graduate school, an increased emphasis on historical thinking means more time in archives, more courses dedicated to the production of publishable articles, less time spent as passive students and more time as active professional historians. Graduate school in history should be structured like a workshop or a cooperative where students learn from real practitioners of the craft. This would encourage professors to keep up their research and to use the cumulative brain power of their classes to conduct large-scale research projects. At all levels, history teachers should be more than teachers; they should also actually be historians, who write and publish their own works. To talk about history, to know what it is, requires active engagement with historical sources.

There are many ways in which historical thinking is gaining ground in classrooms and in general scholarship as teachers push back against the testing bureaucracy to incorporate their own stories and lessons, and as graduate students and history professors assert their right to be independent, creative thinkers. On the web and in print, there are an increasing number of examples of creative historical thinking. On the Internet, arguments about history play with vehemence and concern for facts and method. As historical topics become fodder for the culture wars (as I am typing this, Confederate war statues are in the news), it forces us to think critically about history and how to apply the lessons of the past. Our increasingly sensitive culture plays into the growth of historical thinking because we recognize the latter as a crucial tool in defending our values. Thinking about the past in critical, creative ways should also help us to relate better to others with whom we disagree and help us recognize the difference between actual irreconcilable disagreement and simple differences of perspectives, poor communication or just misunderstanding of each other's view.

Creative History Education as Play for Social Ends

To increase our focus on creative historical thinking, we need to play more and worry less about the judgment and condemnation of our peers. Play is experimentation, a willing openness to potential failure. What is the most memorable thing you learned in history class? For most of us, the answer is some participatory exercise. In fifth grade, I remember students paired off and we marched towards each other until we could see the whites of the other person's eyes, like the American soldiers waiting to fire their guns at the Battle of Bunker Hill. Friends of mine remember building a model garrison or a wigwam reconstruction. Visits to historic sites imprint visual memories and an understanding of the spatial dimensions and physical characteristics of old homes, forts, battlefields, etc.

The key to good historical education at all levels is to allow students the freedom to be creative and imaginative, to seek out their own interests and discover history for themselves, but in cooperation with others. When I was in elementary school, an art teacher told me that to make art, I needed to use my imagination. Under her watchful eyes, I never felt comfortable expressing myself. If my artwork was poor, I took it as a sign that I just didn't have enough imagination. The teacher praised another student for his imagination, so I copied him. The directive to "use more imagination" in art class, or the similar injunction to "provide more analysis" in a history class, is meaningless if students do not first understand what *imagination* or *analysis* is. The art teacher might as well have told me that the artwork needed more magic. The creative imagination of the historian, however, is different from the imagination of the artist. The historian's imagination is a kind of paradigmatic imagination or intuition, which, in the words of Jerome Bruner, is "the ability to see possible formal connections before one is able to prove them in any way."[1] Bruner suggests that in the humanities, we must constantly generate hypotheses, not to test or falsify them like in the hard sciences, but to fit them to conceivable experience, to recognize their verisimilitude.[2] The historical imagination, then, allows the historian to seek patterns. Analysis is the process of discovering and explaining patterns.

History education should be open to all varieties of history from the profoundly political to the antiquarian, from local and regional history to national and world history. It should include history in both the short and the long terms. Furthermore, we should learn about the nature of history and how other people experience the past so that we can understand how people can share in historical knowledge yet disagree about historical interpretation. I think we need a creative historians' code, something like this:

> On my honor, I will do my best, to not be just a chronicler or plagiarist. I promise not to write another unnecessary biography of a founding father. I promise to help genealogists even when I don't really want to. I promise always to be curious, to be dutiful in my footnoting, and never fail to listen to multiple sides of a story.

Because creativity begins with curiosity and develops through play, creative historical thinking must include a bit of fun. After much practice, creative historical thinking becomes natural. When we find the solution to a puzzle, or to a chess match, or any problem whatsoever, the solution seems obvious. In his study of creativity, Arthur Koestler noted that the more original a discovery was, the more it seemed to be obvious after it was discovered. The synthesis of ideas "looks deceptively self-evident, and does not betray the imaginative effort needed to put its component parts together."[3] When we close ourselves to creativity, we fail to encounter those "Aha!" moments, those "Eurekas!" Without creativity in history, society is stagnant.

There is too often a false choice presented between history that is applied to present problems and history for its own sake. History, by its very definition cannot be for its own sake, but rather it is for a purpose or meaning that a historian intends and an audience interprets. History is always applied. For political and religious reasons, many people want history to be taught in one way, from one perspective that they deem true and comfortable. But history doesn't teach us all the same lessons, and it doesn't teach us equally. It can't teach the same lessons because we all encounter our own challenges and need to find particular answers. History doesn't teach one overarching lesson because we don't even know what ultimate question to ask. Historical knowledge doesn't necessarily make us smarter or allow us to predict the future with much accuracy, but it does give us wisdom through examples that we can apply in similar situations. So, we can warn about the potentialities of the future by asking others to mind the past.

History, if done right, has a way of bringing us together—and we must be its architects, using history for good purpose. But writing good history takes work and imagination to find common ground. Historical knowledge is a kind of chaotic knowledge that swirls around us and interacts with us all in different ways. Each person, each family, each community has a unique history, and each of these histories matters. History is justified because people's experiences matter. To capture and explain these experiences, though, we need to imagine alternatives to linear history, to nationalistic narratives, and to standard accounts. Only then can we better understand and explain the past in new, creative, and inclusive ways.

Memorizing specific factoids and dates of major events from the past does not necessarily make you a better person. But learning to think about history in a fuller way will, I believe, make you a better person, more sympathetic to others, more critical in your analysis, more skeptical of standing interpretations, and more knowledgeable of the world. We do not have access to pure reality, but only filtered reality. History is not rote memorization of the past; it is a process of creative and critical reconstruction of the past in which we seek meaningful patterns from a multitude of perspectives.

Notes

1. Jerome Bruner, *Actual Minds, Possible Words* (Cambridge, MA: Harvard University Press, 1986), 13.
2. Bruner, *Actual Minds*, 52.
3. Arthur Koestler, *The Act of Creation* (New York: Macmillan, 1964), 658.

Appendix A
Common Questions College Students Ask About History

Question #1: I really like history. Should I go to grad school in history?

Nine times out of ten, my answer to this question is only one word that is two letters long. If you want to spend two years getting a masters' degree and another four to eight getting a doctorate, liking history is not enough to see you through. To become a professional historian, you should be eternally curious and interested in ideas and arguments. You should be determined, even stubborn, competitive, and ambitious. In graduate school, you can't study something so broad as all of World War Two, or the entire Civil War. Instead, you need to specialize and focus on a smaller topic. Yet, given the nature of academia, not all potential topics will be on the table. For example, there are very few places where you can study to be a historian of Indonesia, or Denmark, or South Africa. Academic history is divided into traditional areas of study, with European and American history the most common subfields. Growing fields of African, Asian, and Latin American history offer a lot of promise for young scholars looking to tread new ground.

Graduate school in history means years of poverty and sacrifice. While your friends are out in the world making real money, you will make just enough to pay for rent and food, if you are lucky. You will probably need to take on some loan debt, which will burden you for decades. You might have to move multiple times for different degrees and for your research. Then, when you apply for a job, you will have little success if you limit yourself to too small a geographic area. This means that at 30–35 years of age, you will have to start over on the opposite side of the country. For adventurous souls, this might not sound so bad.

History graduate programs require a lot of reading and writing. A masters' degree will help prepare you for certain jobs, but almost no universities these days will hire someone without a Ph.D. to teach for them, except perhaps for poor pay on a course-by-course basis as an adjunct instructor. Once you accept adjunct work, you will have a difficult time finding a full-time position. This is in part because working as an adjunct sends a signal to potential employers that you are willing to work for less. Adjunctivitis is a kind of disease whose symptoms include lack of upward mobility. Ironically, a doctorate is a research degree that primarily makes teachers, since there are far too few research professorships. A career in history usually requires you to be able to both lecture and produce research, although there are jobs where you can do just one or the other.

Now, if you have come this far in this book, and still think you want to go to graduate school, I can offer a glimmer of hope. A career of the mind, a lifetime spent reading and writing history, is an incredible privilege that is rarely matched. If you study consistently and network, you will be able to find a job somewhere, doing something related to history. If you are a talented researcher and writer and you put your heart and soul into the discipline, you have a decent chance of becoming a professor. But there are also many other rewarding jobs in public history (museums, archives, etc.) that may be available.

Probably the most important thing that can happen on your road to becoming a historian is that people tell you "no," or they tell you that you might not be good enough. If you respond to that kind of rejection by doubling your efforts, if you are the kind of person who can apply yourself for the long term, and if you are incredibly good at delaying gratification, then this might be a path for you.

Question #2: How do historians make money? If you get a history degree, do you have to become a teacher or a professor? What other jobs can you get with a history degree?

Sometimes, historians don't make money. Most of them, I suppose, teach in K–12 or in colleges and universities. Some historians can make money by writing books and articles, but free-lancing as a historian is incredibly difficult, and there are only a handful of historians in the country who can make a decent living from book sales alone. Historians work as archivists, museum registrars, and curators. They also work for government agencies.

No degree will automatically get you or guarantee you a job, and no discipline will necessarily make you hard-working or more intelligent. History departments across the country are guilty of overselling the discipline by playing up the job potential for future gradates. The truth is, if you want a solid career, you should study accounting or finance or economics, and if you still want to write history, do so on the side. Although I have misgivings about the pecuniary value of a history degree, I think history is a good discipline for preparation in a variety of fields. One reason for this is that research skills learned as a historian are transferrable even when content isn't. After all, the book's message is largely a positive message. That is, history is a form of problem solving, a bisociative discipline that is the combination of all other disciplines. What you gain from a history education is the knowledge of where to look for information, and how to stay on the trail of the evidence. You learn to write, to argue persuasively, and to recognize alternative viewpoints. A history education helps you become an independent researcher. It builds confidence that you can discover new things and become an expert on a topic. But history education is also a social discipline, that helps you learn to work with others and rely on others (like archivists, librarians, co-authors, and journal referees, for example).

A history education can be useful in everything from law to journalism to business, but the connection to such a career will not always be immediately obvious. You have to be careful not to think that all history majors are successful, since this is the image that you might get if you attend a history conference or read a publication of the nation's largest historical organization, the American Historical Association. The history department at Harvard recently published a booklet called "What to Do With History" which includes career summaries from perhaps one hundred former history "concentrates" (they don't call them "majors" at Harvard).[1] If you listen to these graduates, it seems anything indeed is possible. Those who didn't become history professors got jobs as lawyers or consultants with places like Goldman Sachs and Morgan Stanley. Most other graduates mentioned analysis skills and research experience as the keys that prepared them for a future outside of history. One graduate was more direct: "The study of history exposed me to centuries of human folly and irony. This helped shape my comedic sensibility." It is obvious that going to good schools matters, and that a Harvard reputation will take you part of the way. But success is dependent to a large degree on how you blaze your own trail. Harvard concentrates generally have some intellectual and financial advantages, but many of them are also good at networking, through which they discover a satisfying position doing something where their training in analysis and writing applies.

It remains the case that too many students who get a bachelor's degree in history, or even a master's degree in the same, have done little to prepare themselves for a career, and their history departments do little to prepare them for the practical challenges of the market for historians. An education in history does not guarantee a job. If you want to work in a field, you can apply your history degree; don't wait until after you graduate. It is up to you to find and cultivate a relationship between what you've learned in a history program and what you intend to do with it in the world. Find an internship or work at an archives or a museum, become a research assistant to a professor, and ask professors for advice about what to read.

The distance between a history education and teaching history is not very far, so that is the easiest divide to bridge. But moving from a history student to a lawyer or a business manager does not always have an obvious link, so you need to look for your niche. Perhaps your training in history will help you research and write articles for a job in marketing with a large company. Maybe your history education will give you the language or cultural knowledge to work in a foreign country, or communicate between countries.

Question #3: Who do you think was the best president? If you could live in the past, what period of history would you want to live in? What historical figure would you most like to meet?

I've listed these questions together because they are of the same nature. They are better questions for history buffs than for historians. Each of these questions betrays the type of simple linear history and fact-based history education that I argued against in chapters two and three, respectively. The first question is the legacy of a school system that overemphasizes political history in the curriculum. Why must we rank presidents? How can such a ranking even be performed? By what measure should we rank them? By administrative excellence, or personality? Any ranking of the presidents is bound to be informed by ideology, or just personal preference for certain personalities. In most rankings, the recent presidents get placed at the top or bottom of the ranking, depending on one's party views. The less-memorable presidents like Milliard Filmore and John Tyler get sandwiched in the middle of the rankings somewhere as an afterthought. War presidents tend to be ranked higher.

Responding to the second part, about where in the past I would like to live, I have a similarly cynical answer. Considering that I can't see anything without corrective lenses, I probably wouldn't want to go back more than a couple hundred years. At any time before the modern era, I'd also be astronomically more likely to die from some terrible disease. That being said, would I like to see the gladiator fights in Rome, you bet! I'd also really like to talk to the last Norse person to have survived in medieval Greenland. That, then, also answers the final question about what historical figure I'd like to meet. By "historical figure," people usually mean someone who is generally recognizable by an educated person today–a figure of Mahatma Gandhi, Julius Caesar, or Teddy Roosevelt quality. A lot of people say that they'd like to meet Churchill, or try to stop Hitler, or get a glimpse of Jesus. I think if I met Winston Churchill, I'd find him to be a ridiculous bore. Who is this out-of-shape old man with his hat, cane, cigar, and three-piece suit? And what is he doing sitting in my office? Well, perhaps I could meet the younger Winston Churchill, but I assume his character then would be much the same. If I went back to stop Hitler, I wouldn't get very far before someone recognized my terrible American accent.

Question #4: Is Wikipedia okay to use as a source in my research paper?

I remember when Wikipedia began back in 2001, in ye olde days of Internet encyclopedias. At the time, there was a lot of push-back against the idea that Wikipedia would be edited by anonymous people on the Internet. The assumption was that no open-source dictionary could ever be as trustworthy as a well-curated professional print encyclopedia like the Encyclopedia Brittanica. This feeling of unease also stemmed, I think, from a lack of trust in digital sources and a reverence for the published page. History teachers everywhere reacted to the arrival of Wikipedia by warning against it, and by using it in examples where its entries had been purposely falsified. Because Wikipedia was then mostly unregulated, and moderators were few and far between, there was a real chance that an entry was corrupted. But, at the same time, there was also the opportunity for creativity and passion to flourish. I recall in particular a very long, creative, and professionally-sounding biographical entry for "Cap'n Crunch," the cartoon figure of the eponymous popular sugary breakfast cereal. The author or authors of the Cap'n Crunch entry had gone to extreme lengths to find all of the old television advertisement footage and physical marketing publications of the Cap'n. They then created an actual historiography, with nuanced, balanced (albeit comical) debates about the origin, life, and accomplishments of the old seafaring cereal legend. The contributors recognized contradictions in the official story given by Quaker Oats (the cereal's manufacturer) and provided possible alternative explanations for events. It was a riot, and a howler of a work. A few years later, when I checked on this biography of the Cap'n, I discovered that it had been severely reworked to bring it into line with the preferences of the Wikipedia moderators.[2] Gone was the historiographical debate, the genius, the comedy. The world was robbed of a stunning masterpiece. Today, Wikipedia is the most used encyclopedia in the world, and it is gaining trust. Encyclopedia Britannica now positions itself as a rival to Wikipedia, calling itself a "fact-checked online encyclopedia," having given up publishing physical volumes. Arguments about Wikipedia preceded by more than a decade the concern with "alternative facts," but they are part of the same discussion about historical thinking, the weighing of evidence, and credulity. People are rightly concerned that entries on Wikipedia are subject to change, so it looks untrustworthy, it looks unsettled, and we can see how unstable it is. In the end, though, the lesson of Wikipedia is that history and description is never a settled business, that we must verify our findings and debate how to present them. We have a right to be suspicious and critical of every source. Children who grew up with Wikipedia recognize this, I think, and so they are well on their way to becoming historians.

Question #5: Isn't history always written by the winners?

Well, apparently you haven't spent much time in the American South, where the neo-Confederate press is an active publisher of works on history. The history of the "Lost Cause" has been a stable feature of the American historical landscape ever since Lee surrendered at Appomattox.

Now, it is true in the most obvious sense that if someone is killed in battle, they are not going to be able to write down their experiences. It is also true that those who win battles and win elections gain positions of power and control therewith the education boards that determine the content of textbooks. Court historians and intelligentsia write histories to justify political power. While these "winners" might control the dominant historical narrative, in any free society, there are also popular alternative voices. Consider Howard Zinn's *A People's History of the United States*, for example, or Thaddeus Russell's *A Renegade History*, both of which get little respect in academic circles but have struck a nerve with readers.

Historically, large powerful groups of people crushed their enemies and burned their books. The Vikings and the Mongols burned and plundered, but it was only the defeated peoples who wrote about these events. In the twentieth century, the Germans lost World War I but then dominated much of the historiography of the event. In the Spanish Civil War, Franco's nationalists were victorious, but the popular history of the struggle was written by the defeated forces. Al Gore lost the U.S. presidential election of 2000, and his supporters are still writing about it.

Even groups that have been victims of genocide produce histories. In a political and historical context, for example, the Jewish people can hardly be considered winners on the world stage. They've endured the Babylonian Exile, a Roman occupation, and the Holocaust. And yet, they are largely responsible for the Bible, perhaps the most influential history book of all time.

Some of the most influential works of history ever written were written by those with marginal positions in society.

Notes

1. Harvard University History Department, "What to Do With History," 2007. https:// history.fas.harvard.edu/files/history/files/whattodowithhistory.pdf, accessed March 21, 2018.
2. Wikipedia, "Cap'n Crunch," n.d. https://en.wikipedia.org/wiki/Cap'n_Crunch (older versions are still available in the page history), accessed March 21, 2018.

Appendix B
The Creative Historian's "Histocratic" Oath

Repeat after me:

I swear by Clio the muse of history, and by Herodotus, Thucydides, Leopold von Ranke, Ken Burns, and Eric Foner that I will carry out, according to my ability and judgment, this oath and indenture.

That I will use my historical knowledge to teach the youth to treat history as a creative discipline through lectures interesting and various, material culture exercises, field trips, debates, and research projects, but never with a view towards requiring them to remember particular facts. Nor will I administer tests that ask merely for the recall of information.

On my honor, I will do my best to not be just a chronicler or plagiarist. I promise not to write another unnecessary biography of a founding father. I promise to help genealogists even when I don't really want to. I promise always to be curious, to be dutiful in my footnoting, and never fail to listen to multiple sides of a story.

Index